"There is perhaps no greater challenge in our personal relationships than conflict. In this wonderfully engaging, perceptive, and wise little book, Diane Musho Hamilton shows us how to negotiate this delicate terrain with skillful means."

—William Ury, coauthor of *Getting to Yes* and author of *The Power of a Positive No*

"A wonderful, down-to-earth, and very useful book on conflict resolution. I had my first 'integral' awakening when I realized that every conflict and seeming opposition was actually an opportunity to find a deeper unity of perspectives, and it is this same leading-edge integral vision that guides Diane's terrific book. Read it professionally, read it as a layperson, read it for work, read it for relationships, read it for your own inner conflicts—but read it for sure, and find a genuine peace and contentment under all of your seemingly intractable conflicts. You'll be delighted you did!"

—Ken Wilber, author of *The Integral Vision: A Very Short Introduction to the Revolutionary Integral Approach to Life, God, the Universe, and Everything*

"A groundbreaking, creative account of how the qualities of nonattachment, equanimity, and flexibility of mind that are cultivated in meditation practice can help inform and enliven the vital work of mediating human conflicts and misunderstandings."

—Jan Chozen Bays, author of *Mindful Eating* and *How to Train a Wild Elephant*

everything is workable

A ZEN APPROACH TO CONFLICT RESOLUTION

Diane Musho Hamilton

Shambhala
BOSTON & LONDON
2013

Shambhala Publications, Inc.
Horticultural Hall
300 Massachusetts Avenue
Boston, Massachusetts 02115
www.shambhala.com

9 8 7 6 5 4 3 2 1

First Edition
Printed in the United States of America

⊗This edition is printed on acid-free paper that meets the
American National Standards Institute Z39.48 Standard.
♻This book is printed on 30% postconsumer recycled paper.
For more information please visit www.shambhala.com.

Distributed in the United States by Penguin Random House LLC
and in Canada by Random House of Canada Ltd

Designed by James D. Skatges

Library of Congress Cataloging-in-Publication Data
Hamilton, Diane Musho.
Everything is workable: a Zen approach to conflict resolution /
Diane Musho Hamilton.—First edition.
    pages   cm
Includes bibliographical references and index.
ISBN 978-1-61180-067-8 (pbk.: alk. paper)
1. Conflict management—Religious aspects—Buddhism.
2. Buddhism—Social aspects. I. Title.
BQ4570.C588H36 2013
294.3'37—dc23
2013009893

To Michael,
who takes the long view...

Contents

Acknowledgments

Many thanks to my good friends and allies, Simon Egan, Dori Them, Julia Sati, Rebecca Colwell, and Rob McNamara, who wanted these talks to be shared and whose enthusiasm and support ensured that this book would come to be; to Marco Morelli, whose early writing and editing gave this project an important bump start, and who helped to flesh out the Integral ideas; to Jeri Schneider, a truly creative friend and editor, who kept the writing process dynamic and insisted on keeping us both laughing throughout; to Jane Goetz, for her keen eye and fine-tuning of the text; to Randee Levine, for her ongoing encouragement and love; and to my friends and partners at the Integral Institute: Jeff Salzman, Terry Patten, Sofia Diaz, Cindy Lou Golin, Huy Lam, Clint Fuhs, Jason Diggs, Decker Cunov, Robert Mac Naughton, Robb Smith, Daviod Riordan, Nicole Fegley, and Kelly Bearer.

Much gratitude to my Shambhala editors David O'Neal, for his interest in this book, encouragement, deft attention, and ever-so-light touch, and John Golebiewski, for his subtle refinements. Thank you to Genpo Roshi for his Big Mind and Zen teaching, and to Ken Wilber for changing my viewpoint and, therefore, my life. Finally, I wish to extend my whole hearted appreciation to my family and husband for their fierce and committed style of love. It is the best.

Introduction

I grew up in the American West between the Rocky Mountains and the Great Basin desert. It was untamed land—vast, rugged, and open. The people who lived there—miners, ranchers, immigrants, Native Americans, and my own extended family—were as beautiful and rough as the landscape.

My mother was one of ten children and a second cousin to Gene Fullmer, former American middleweight boxer and world champion; her family was known as the Fighting Fullmers. She was named "the Tempest in a Teapot" in her high school yearbook because of her unbridled temper and compulsive tendency to stick up for the underdogs. She was kicked off her school bus after scolding the driver for dropping off a girl in a snowbank, and she spent the rest of the year riding the boys' bus home.

Her family was highly expressive, and temperamental, filled with deep sensitivity and a lot of unresolved pain. But they were also fun. On holidays, all nine of my aunts and uncles and a smattering of in-laws would gather at my grandmother's house for full days of conversation, banter, and laughter. By 9:00 P.M., the talking, teasing, and joking were lively; by one in the morning, the arguments were heating up, and by three, someone was likely to storm out the front door threatening never to come back. That is, if they hadn't been thrown out earlier.

These clashes rarely turned into estrangements. In my family, the bonding was deep, and we shook off the fights like a bear shakes off a skirmish with a big cat. We seemed to understand that there was little in life we could count on except one another, so we hung together through thick and thin, up and down. And like Keith Richards said of the Rolling Stones, we are still together because "we knew how to patch it up."

Believe me, there were lots of times when I personally would have preferred that—as Rodney King implored—we could all just get along. Perhaps that we would take the time to listen respectfully to each other's point of view. Or relinquish a moment of emotional intensity for a few minutes of peace. Or drop an argument or disagreement because it really didn't matter. There was pain in our fighting; it stressed our nervous systems and burdened our hearts the way separation, long or short, always does.

Nonetheless, there was life force in it and, strangely, a lot of care. People's truths poured forth, their feelings rushed out, and while there were moments when we said things we may have regretted later—well, at least you always knew where you stood. I was compelled to try to understand and work with the challenge of my family's style of engagement. I remember the distinct experience of being a rapt bystander to some intense arguments, sensing the powerful intimacy and, at the same time, the danger of the emotional intensity, while also seeing the contradictory truth of each position. Naturally, I didn't want to take sides, but as far as I could tell, everyone was right, even though everyone was also wrong.

I noticed that, when I was involved, I was as intractable and self-righteous as everyone else. I furiously set about asserting my opinions, insisting I was right, trying to build a coalition of support for my point of view, often to no avail. But the contradictions, the feelings, and the emotional engagement compelled me to keep watching, listening, and wondering. Those early experiences led to my work as a mediator later in life because I was so interested in this territory of conflict. I knew what it meant to be lost in the fray. I knew what it felt like to be misunderstood or furious, to be an ally in someone else's fight, or to sit back as an unbiased and neutral observer.

Six months after I turned seventeen, my focus changed abruptly. Seven of my friends died: four in a plane crash, one in a car rollover, one in a knife fight, and one by suicide. In the face of so much death, my attention quickly turned from curiosity about anger and passion in relationships to life's great existential questions. What is the meaning of our existence? Who am I? Who are we? What is love in the face of certain death?

I came to see that anything short of resolving these questions was insufficient, so I became a committed student of meditation. The practice of sitting still and concentrating the mind and body in the present moment scratched a peculiar itch in me. It allowed me to access an essential peace, to include all that, as Rilke said, "was unresolved in my heart," and revealed a deep satisfaction in the way things are. I began to see that the first, essential step in real conflict resolution is realizing the place of inherent peace in oneself.

And yet, the relationship work has to be done. It is one of our evolutionary assignments, along with addressing other big-ticket items, such as economic justice, basic human rights, and environmental sustainability. We have much to learn about how to curb the frequent outbreaks of violence and warfare that have been so devastating in our collective history. We need to learn how to reliably transform our conflicts into opportunity and creativity, and to develop solid methods for helping people around the world get along.

Personal conflict resolution practice is one of the best ways to contribute to this collective goal. When we directly face our own overwhelming fear of/in relationships and start to change our ill-adapted ways of coping with conflict, we become braver and more confident. We taste the possibility of living in authentic relationships that are both enlivened and intimate. We come to understand that good relationships require practice like everything else. We actually experience how a few simple skills can make a big difference in helping with these challenges, and we naturally become more open and more daring in working things out with our close friends and family.

Let's face it. We human beings are a compelling mix. We are highly cooperative and highly competitive. We are peace loving and volatile, warmongering and altruistic, pragmatic and foolish. When we love, we love. And when we fight, it takes a toll. But rather than relying on a thin, idealized hope that we will all one day just get along, we can approach conflict resolution as an art form that we are privileged to develop and hone. We can accept the challenge, becoming adept in transforming our personal struggles, and contribute to the unfolding of new ways of being for humanity.

everything is workable

1

Conflict Is Good News

Love wants to reach out and manhandle us,
Break all our teacup talk of God.
HAFIZ[1]

MOST OF US DON'T LIKE CONFLICT. Usually, the conflicts we experience in our lives seem unfortunate and unnecessary, a disturbance to our peace and a waste of our precious time and energy. There are times when they become painfully destructive. If you have ever been estranged from a lover or friend, lost a business partner over a financial disagreement, or been driven from your home by political turmoil, you know how wrenching these upheavals are.

The simple, self-evident truth is that, however difficult, conflict is intrinsic to our human experience—in other words, it isn't going away. It is part of the rich, gritty, and indispensable stuff of our lives. Every great novel, film, or memorable story revolves around conflict. Shakespeare's great tragedies could not have been written without the intrigue and treachery, nor would they instruct us in the deep truths of human life.

The Buddha is known for his insight, serenity, and nonattachment, but his own life journey, like that of Jesus, was highly engaged with others and the challenges of conflict. After his awakening, the Buddha became a great spiritual teacher and also a leader to a community of practitioners. He advised the political leaders of his time, mediating and negotiating treaties on their behalf. In other words, the Buddha engaged fully in the world with others, acting politically and dealing with the challenges that arose in his own community.

A little-known part of his story is that at the end of his life, a war broke out between his clan and the neighboring one across the river over water rights, and his entire village was destroyed. I wonder what that was like for someone with such great realization. He had taught his followers to deeply accept the conditions of life, not to resist or cling to ideas of how they wished the world would be. He practiced accepting reality on its terms and working with it directly, manifesting wisdom and compassion in ever-changing circumstances. But he must have also been very sad.

His Holiness the Dalai Lama is another example of someone who exemplifies the equanimity of spiritual practice while working with intractable, long-term conflict. As a spiritual leader, he also maintains the difficult political task of leading Tibetans in exile and working to influence China and the rest of the world on their behalf. Mahatma Gandhi and Martin Luther King, Jr., are other role models of deep spiritual discipline and political skill, as are Nelson Mandela, Desmond Tutu, and Aung San Suu Kyi.

While our own challenges may seem insignificant by comparison, they aren't. When we have a conflict with those around us, we are given an opportunity to practice transforming that conflict into patience, mutual understanding, and creativity. When we use the opportunity, we contribute to the shared endeavor of learning how to live peacefully with each other. This is one of the greatest challenges of the global human community, and each one of our individual efforts makes a difference in our collective evolution.

From Crisis to Possibility

To learn to transform conflict, we must let go of the notion that something or someone is wrong or bad. This belief creates fundamental resistance, and it is the first obstacle to working with conflict. We can shift our point of view to see that conflicts, like dreams, may possess an elegant intelligence that expresses truths we may not want to see clearly. For example, an old pattern needs to be abandoned or a relationship needs to grow or change. We can, with practice, learn to see this intelligence at work and respond creatively and constructively. The conflict isn't the problem; our response to it is.

When a conflict erupts in our lives, it has the potential to invigorate us, to disrupt our habitual patterns, and to compel us to learn something new. Conflicts interrupt life as usual, and we are catapulted into the unknown, into a space of open possibility filled with electric tension.

When I was in college, I fell in love. For six months it was bliss, and we were completely dedicated to pleasing each other. All of a sudden the bliss became irritation. The very intimacy we enjoyed turned against us. Irritability set in, then claustrophobia. In a naive attempt to catch our breath, we broke up.

When I look back, I see how much wisdom there was in our conflict. The conflict expressed the truth of our overcommunion, and it summoned us to regain a balance that included others. We needed to grow out of our loving cocoon, but at that point, we didn't know how. We simply moved apart.

The opportunity for change can be personal and collective. If you think back to 2001 after the attacks on the World Trade Center and before the invasion of Afghanistan, there was a period of time when the world was experiencing the trauma and sadness directly, without retaliation or counterattack from the United States.

In that open space, it seemed like something new might be possible. People were experiencing an awful truth—the way humans attack and kill others over differences in power and worldview. We were outraged, heartbroken, and stunned, but we were also asking questions: What motivated the attackers? How did U.S. foreign policy contribute? What was the best way for the nation to respond?

During that time, many of us were propelled into emotional disequilibrium as we shifted perspectives, looking for insight. We identified with a nation and city that had just been attacked, imagining the last moments of the victims who died and their phone calls to their families. We tried to glimpse what motivated the attackers who flew the planes into the buildings and the mind of the terrorist organizations that trained them. We considered the options of political leaders and military strategists, and we empathized with the innocent bystanders of the world—nations and individuals alike—who longed for either revenge or peaceful resolution.

This questioning opened the possibility of responding differently. Whether we, as people and a culture, responded from necessity, clarity, or habitual pattern is debatable, but there was an opening nonetheless. Similar opportunities arise in our personal lives, and the conflicts that generate those possibilities can serve as drivers to our development. We learn how to listen, consider other ways of seeing, reexamine our own assumptions and deeply held beliefs, and expand our worldviews.

I have a close friend—a spiritual companion, you might say—whom I have known for more than twenty years. We both have sons with Down syndrome. We've been through a lot together, navigating the grief, prejudice, and isolation of having a child with a disability. We've supported each other through thick and thin, the easy and difficult times.

As our sons approached adulthood, I began to notice a shortness between us and an edge of irritability in our conversations. It became more and more uncomfortable until there came a point when we just had to talk about it. I didn't particularly want to; approaching these kinds of conversations isn't fun. But we finally had our spontaneous come-to-Jesus meeting.

After navigating a flurry of hurt feelings and considerable tension, we realized that the tension between us was a result of our sons reaching adulthood and that our paths had to grow in different directions. We were both sad and fearful of facing the future without each other. But our conversation helped us bring awareness, understanding, and compassion to the changes, while we discovered other ways to support each other.

Learning how to negotiate conflict demands that we become more present, more fearless. Consequently, we may need to relinquish the hopeful image of ourselves as remaining serene under all circumstances, like sitting buddhas carved from wood or stone. We have to expect our composure to be compromised as we learn about the possibilities and creative solutions of working directly with the conflict in our relationships. Even, and maybe especially, when things don't turn out as we want, our engagement with discord refines and teaches us, sometimes altering our life's very course.

Whether the results are invigorating or devitalizing depends on how consciously we work with ourselves and our circumstances. Simply retreating, smoothing things over, or trying to win out won't take us to anyplace new. Developing our skills creates a sense of freedom; a confidence in ourselves; and an ability to be real, intimate, and ultimately loving with others.

Remember, if we had no disagreements with the world, we would have little reason to grow and less opportunity to become more compassionate, wakeful human beings. Like the Buddha or the Dalai Lama, we can develop the skills to work with conflicts and reliable methods as a human community to transform them. Our ability to transform our conflicts on a personal level will eventually lead to a shared ability to create a more peaceful and harmonious world. It is our challenge, our privilege, and our destiny in an evolving world.

PRACTICE

View of Conflict

Reflect on a conflict that comes up in your life this week. Ask yourself a few questions about it, giving yourself permission to explore:

1. What are the circumstances, and what are your judgments about the conflict? Does it feel wrong or bad? Do you believe that the other person is at fault?
2. Is there anything that is right about the conflict? In other words, can you see intelligence in the conflict?
3. What truth or truths does the conflict express?
4. How will you grow by working with the conflict instead of resisting or avoiding it?

2

Inner Peace, Outer Peace

Without inner peace, outer peace is impossible. We all wish
for world peace, but it will never be achieved unless we first
establish peace within our own minds.

GESHE KELSANG GYATSO[1]

THE TEACHER IS SPEAKING a fundamental truth here, one that we
sense intuitively. When we look around, we see that the great con-
temporary heroes of world peace—Nelson Mandela, Desmond Tutu,
His Holiness the Dalai Lama, Thich Nhat Hanh, and Aung San Suu
Kyi—all exude a profound sense of inner peace. The depth that they
convey through their presence is the most persuasive part of their
message for social harmony and justice. They are real-life examples
of internal depth, resilience, and harmony in spite of living through
terrible social discord and political strife—conditions they have cou-
rageously endured and committed their lives to changing. If His Holiness radiates true peace in spite of sixty years of exile from Tibet, if
Mandela smiles with broad, unassuming genuineness after more than
twenty-five years of imprisonment in South Africa, if Aung San Suu

Kyi still expresses grace and confidence after twenty years of house arrest in Burma, the rest of us can be encouraged by their example to find a source of well-being that extends beyond our current conflicts and daily life challenges.

We sense that the true source of our peace is to be found right where we are. As Zen Master Dogen says, "If you can't find the truth right where you are, where do you expect to find it?" This insight draws us instinctively toward the practice of sitting meditation. But anyone who has spent any time on a cushion knows that our early experiences may not reveal the depth of peace we are searching for.

The first encounter with ourselves is often an unruly mix of bodily discomfort, emotional unease, and unchecked commentary from the discursive mind, that anxious and unsettling voice inside each of us. Buddhist texts often refer to this voice as the "monkey mind," that stream of uninvited thoughts that perpetually swings unchecked through our awareness. These thoughts are noisy, distracting, even menacing as they call out our fears, regrets, frustrations, desires, angers, and concerns. Indeed, our interior is far from peaceful; it is a jungle in there.

Ego

At the center of all this noise is the voice of the ego or small self. The word *ego* in Greek means simply "I." When we sit, we begin to notice the constancy of our preoccupation with the self. We evaluate whether we are safe, whether we are successful, whether the world is treating us fairly. From one point of view, our self-concern makes sense. It is our responsibility to look after ourselves, to find ways to be happy and involved in life. But when we pay close attention, we find that the discursive mind sounds more like an interview from an episode of *Survivor.* We report feeling very unsafe, exposed, and insecure in a dangerous and competitive world. Our mind is filled with thoughts about the people and situations that threaten us. We look forward and then back over our shoulders as we strive to protect ourselves, our image, and our future.

Even in the most positive circumstances, when we are surrounded by people we love in a familiar environment, the struggle of the ego continues. It moves from the struggle of basic survival to the struggle of constant improvement—striving to be wealthier, more successful, more famous. From the outside we may look more prosperous, but there doesn't seem to be an end to the stress we feel inside—to the coping and striving—and, consequently, to the dissatisfaction that is part of our day-to-day existence.

Noisy and unsatisfied, the small talk of self fills us with tension. The ego is also dualistic, casting everything in opposition—you and me, this and that, right and wrong, good and bad—and the tension in our mind runs between two poles: "I like this, and I don't like that." "I want this, but I don't want that." "I hope for this, but I fear that." Sometimes mundane, sometimes dramatic, our mind oscillates back and forth between, for example, praising ourselves and putting others down, then in the next breath, inflating others and denigrating ourselves. Our mind becomes a litany of yes and no, for and against. We are preoccupied with comparisons, forming so many opinions, judgments, and preferences in reaction to life that rarely do we simply allow ourselves to experience things just as they are.

By becoming aware of this internal voice and its messages, we can learn to shape our mind in a more constructive way. A therapist or coach can support us in moderating self-criticism, decreasing the intensity of our judgments, healing the regrets of the past, and overcoming our fear of the future. But a healthy, functional ego still relies on the fundamental division between the self and the world. As long as we are limited to this perspective, we will experience the tension of this division. To find the kind of peace the Buddha talks about, we must learn to quiet the mind altogether. True, settled peace comes when we experience reality without division.

Meditation

The practice of meditation is simple. It is the total concentration of body and mind in relaxed, upright sitting posture. It doesn't take any special skills or talent. We have everything we need to pull up a cushion and sit down; cross our legs; take a full, deep breath; and focus our attention on the here and now. We usually begin with a concentration practice, such as following the breath. We maintain focus on the breath while allowing thoughts, sensations, and feeling states to pass through our awareness like clouds floating across the sky. As our practice stabilizes, we become identified not with the usual parade of thoughts, emotions, or bodily sensations, but with the open space of awareness that pervades all of our experience.

Ultimately, sitting is not about developing concentration, about becoming better at anything. As one master puts it, "It is a gate of ease and joy." Imagine that. It seems too simple to be true. But when the mind settles down and we become one with our immediate experience, our struggle drops away. We are completely present with the here and now; the past is not our concern, and the future does not exist. Everything around us becomes more vivid, more detailed, and interestingly enough, more workable. The grasping and striving of the small-self voice disappears, and we see reality as the whole of Being itself: vivid and distinct, yet whole. Completely still, yet changing. A powerful feeling of well-being ensues, of peacefulness that doesn't depend on anything we have accomplished or done. We taste a fulfillment that is intrinsic to Being itself. We may start to notice that our state of well-being naturally extends outward. Our heart expands, compassion opens naturally like blossoms in spring, and others are included in our best wishes. We enjoy a wide-ranging sense of freedom, and creativity occurs spontaneously.

In his bestseller *The Power of Now,* Eckhart Tolle defines enlightenment as simply "your natural state of *felt* oneness with Being. It is a state of connectedness with something immeasurable and indestructible, something that, almost paradoxically, is essentially you and yet, is much greater than you. It is finding your true nature beyond name and form."[2]

Once we have experienced this capacity for freedom and peace, we might wonder what the struggle was all about. My Zen teacher, Genpo Roshi, gave me the Zen name Musho, which means "no conflict, no struggle." This name reminds me that without division of the mind, there is no struggle. Without division, everything is right here. Without division, there is no separate identity with its worrying and fretting. Without division, there is no effort. Without division, we just are. We are free, compassionate, and creative.

The Importance of Practice and the Birth of Willie

The value of regular meditation became clear to me the first few months after the birth of my son. Willie was born on New Year's Day in 1989. He was my first child. I had been practicing meditation for about seven years, but it wasn't until after his birth that the words "here and now" took on tremendous relevance.

Labor began on New Year's Eve, while I was dining out with my husband. The small tugs of early evening turned into seriously challenging contractions later in the night. Six or seven hours after the onset of labor, a raw life force took over, overwhelming my body in deep, evolutionary purpose. I focused intently on my breathing just to stay present, but nature was in charge. Any thoughts or preferences were extraneous. Birth, like death, was happening according to its own timing and intelligence.

After fourteen hours of labor, my midwife helped bring the baby into the world. My senses were so heightened that every image, feeling, and perception from that moment are etched into my memory. I remember the tenderness in my husband's blue eyes, the pale afternoon light through the window, the capable movements of the woman helping me. I felt the typical overwhelming joy and relief that comes with the dramatic moment of birth. But I also saw a look of concern pass over the midwife's face like a shadow passing over a lake.

I looked at my new baby, and his face was purple. Suddenly I wondered whether he was breathing. "Laurine," I said, "what are you worried about?" She said, "I'm worried about how he looks." I looked at him again. He wasn't crying the way newborns do, and this time I saw a subtle, unusual fold in the shape of his eyes. "Oh, you guys," I said to my husband and family. "He's a Down's baby."

A quiet poignancy settled over the room. Nobody said anything except my younger brother, who leaned down and whispered in my ear, "I love you." As the midwife handed my baby to me, my mind was stunned, and my heart was so raw it ached inside my chest. I guess you could say it was broken. My husband and family quietly left the room, each looking for their own meaning in this event and leaning on each other for comfort. For a little while, I was alone with my baby, stunned and yet still marveling at the brand-new life. I kept hearing the words of the Third Chinese Patriarch in my head, "The Great Way is not difficult for those who have no preferences."

Over the next days and weeks, I went through many emotional ups and downs. The enormous physical changes in my body, the demands of taking care of a newborn, and the unpredictable bouts of fear and grief that accompany having a baby with a disability—those memories are still with me. But because of my meditation practice, I saw very quickly that my uneasy thoughts were almost always about the future—whether my son would be accepted, whether he would ever live on his own, and even whether he would have a girlfriend one day. These thoughts took me immediately into a world of uncertainty, anxiety, and dread. Very quickly, I was able to identify how this future focus was affecting me, and I disciplined my mind to stay present in the here and now.

This was an easy shift to make in the company of a baby. Babies are so simple and present, and they have a magical way of compelling all of our attention. Nothing quite compares to the charisma of a baby for focusing our attention. Their faces are so open and pure, and the simple tasks of feeding, changing, bundling, and taking short walks are natural forms of meditation. Focused on the care of a little one, our mind is freed somewhat of the ego's demands, and things quiet down. Everything is simply what it is, without evaluating or preferring, and life is inherently satisfying. I was blown away by the stark contrast between the moments when I was present and those moments when my mind wandered to the future.

Occasionally, a bout of grief would arise unexpectedly. Once, when I was swimming laps, I cried for forty minutes in the water. When the tears came, they were confusing because I was in love with my new child. I finally realized that I was grieving for the other baby, the one I had thought I would have but didn't. After that, I simply allowed the painful feelings to come and go, and they left me feeling tenderhearted, open, and strangely appreciative. After a while, I felt more compassionate toward the fear and uncertainty, and at times, this compassion seemed to reach out in all directions to include anyone who was suffering.

I look back on that time as one of the deepest practice periods of my life. I learned so much about the freedom and peace of a still mind, when we are simply present with things as they are. I accessed the absolute value of life as it is, with all of its disappointments, trauma, and unexpected difficulties. My hunch is that this is why His Holiness still radiates, why Mandela still smiles, and why Aung San Suu Kyi still expresses grace, despite all they have endured.

Most of us can't imagine what it would be like to live through an invasion, grow up in an apartheid regime, or watch as our family, friends, and neighbors are killed. Yet we also suffer injustices. We are treated unfairly, and tragedies befall us. When these things happen and our world is in chaos, meditation is a sure method to help us access a deep sense of inner calm and trust in the unfolding of our life, in spite of the struggle. And it is a tried-and-true support to us while we learn about other tools so we can work with our life challenges differently.

Many years later, when Willie was about eight, he was sitting in the bathtub while I was getting ready to leave for the day. I walked in, and in the hurried voice of the mother who is late for work, I asked him, "Willie, what are your jobs today?" He looked up serenely from his bath, and pouring water lyrically from a cup back into the tub, he said, "Now."

PRACTICE

Meditation

1. Find a quiet place to sit, putting aside distractions.
2. Sit on a soft, round meditation cushion, crossing your legs. Make sure your knees are below your hips and create a stable base to your posture.
3. You may sit in either the half-lotus or full lotus position—or with your feet placed on the floor, adjacent to each other. For the full lotus, put your right foot on your left thigh and your left foot on your right thigh. For the half-lotus, put your left foot on your right thigh.
4. Place your right hand on your left foot and your left hand on your right hand, with the ends of the thumbs lightly touching each other. With your hands in this position, place them close to your body so the joined thumb tips are at your navel.
5. Straighten your body and sit upright. Your ears should be in line with your shoulders and your nose in line with your navel.
6. Rest your tongue against the roof of your mouth, and breathe through your nose. Your lips and teeth should be closed. Your eyes should be open in a soft gaze resting a few feet in front of you on the floor.
7. Take a breath and exhale fully. Relax.
8. Now just sit, allowing your thoughts to come and go without clinging. Don't judge them or chase them away. Bring your attention to the breath, stay present, and identify yourself with Being, with Awareness, or with Now.

3

Intention: The True North

Intention is the core of all conscious life.
Conscious intention colors and moves everything.
MASTER HSING YUN[1]

MANY PEOPLE THESE DAYS are speaking to us of the importance of intention. They say that when we set a firm intention, we can accomplish great things. With a clear motive and sustained practice, we can quiet the discursive mind and relinquish the mental or emotional habits that cause our suffering. We can become present and awake, responding compassionately to ourselves and others. And finally, we can appreciate our lives just as they are, without obscuring—through countless unmet expectations and inevitable disappointments—our natural capacity for happiness.

Intention can be described as an internal choice or commitment that guides our actions toward something greater than ourselves. The Buddha's original intention was to look into the disturbing truths of old age, sickness, and death, and to find an end to suffering. After six years of dedicated practice, he became enlightened. That is to say, he experienced himself as radically unconditioned awareness, with no sense of separation from anything. He was whole and complete, at one with reality. As he put it to his old friends when he ran into them later, "I am awake."

I knew a sailor once whose life was transformed by an intention. He was in deep pain, and everything was so difficult that he wanted to end his life. One night in great despair, he set sail alone into the North Sea. Instead of throwing himself into the icy, dark water, he looked up to the stars for help. In that moment, he made a vow to Orion to find a way to heal his life. And, over time, he did, with the constellation as his steady, committed witness.

I knew another man, a true force of nature. When, as a child, he looked around the world at the rich and the poor, he decided it was better to be rich. So he intended, this boy of ten, to "build up a big pile of coconuts." He is worth about a billion dollars today. I am not sure he is happy, but his intention wasn't to become happy. It was to become rich. He doubtless likes having money, but making and keeping it includes a lot of stress and competition, so his happiness is not the kind of unconditioned happiness that the Buddha discovered.

Law of Attraction

Many people are talking about the power of intention—from scientifically trained field theorists to New Thought leaders to lovers of the movie *The Secret*. The fundamental principle in most of these teachings is that we will attract what we intend. It is, therefore, essential to be fully aware of our intentions, because we will get what we wish for. On the other hand, when life doesn't give us what we want, we can question why not and unearth the contradictory motives, underlying fears, or beliefs that may have gotten in the way.

There is a deep truth here, and at the same time, many of us are uneasy watching *The Secret*. It doesn't seem to account for the misery and failures in the world, smacking instead of a fantasy of omnipotence whose roots we remember from childhood. It reminds us of the time we first learned about the power of prayer and thought it was a sure avenue to a pony. Inevitably, we experienced some disappointments when our prayers didn't bring concrete results.

So what is the difference between childlike wishful thinking and creative self-determination in a responsive and generous universe?

Here is one more inspiring story to help us sort this out: Recently, I met a remarkable, beautiful Persian woman. As a child in Iran, she slept outside. Gazing up at the stars, she decided she wanted to go up there, to space. She left Iran, went to college in the States, and eventually became an engineer. With her husband, she founded a technology company that generated millions. After they sold it, she used some of the proceeds to become one of the founders of the X PRIZE, a competition to inspire research and spacecraft development for space exploration. You may have heard of her. Her name is Anousheh Ansari.

She got her wish to go to space. Even as she was helping to establish the prize, she applied and was accepted into the Russian space program. She trained as an understudy to a Russian cosmonaut who, due to illness, couldn't make the flight when the time came. In 2006, Anousheh took his place and became one of the first women to experience space flight.

Asked what she hoped to achieve on her flight, she said, "I hope to inspire everyone—especially young people, women, and young girls all over the world, and in Middle Eastern countries that do not provide women with the same opportunities as men—to not give up their dreams. It may seem impossible to them at times. But I believe they can realize their dreams if they keep them in their hearts, nurture them, look for opportunities, and make those opportunities happen."[2]

From the point of view of wholeness, the sailor was healed the very moment he made his intention. Making the promise to Orion was already an expression from the part of him that was healthy.

When Anousheh gazed up at the stars and formed her intention, she entered into an intimacy with space and the stars, which eventually led her to space flight. But, she says, we must create opportunity and make things happen. My friend the capitalist had to maintain his intention and do a great number of business deals before he became as wealthy as he is today. And I am sure the sailor went through many difficult moments on his way to a full recovery.

Intention is a finite commitment, and it is also a process that requires our love and attention. In the beginning, it expresses a true possibility in our world. In the middle, we must clarify it, uproot contradictory motives, realign it with new realities, and apply energy at opportune moments. In the end, our intentions create powerful results. The old adage "Be careful what you wish for" reminds us to be sure that our intentions will bring us what we truly desire. As the Buddha says, "Have few desires, but have great ones."

Clarifying Intention in Communication

If we establish our intention to be as awake as possible, it soon extends to our communication with others. We find that we want to be more engaged with the people in our lives. We aspire to give and receive in a true figure eight of belonging and authenticity.

Whenever I work with people on new communication patterns, I always ask them what their intention is before we start. Do they want to express a perspective or prove a point? Are they interested in listening, or is it more important to have their opinion heard? Are they simply interested in an exchange of views, or do they want to forge a solution? You would be surprised how often problems arise because we aren't clear or even conscious about what we really intend in our interactions with others.

When we fail to recognize our intention while we are communicating, it is like driving blind. We follow old roadways of talking and listening, without knowing where we are going or what we are looking for. How often in the course of a conversation have you heard the expression, "That's not what I meant." It is like coming upon a road sign that says Dead End.

We often engage in social conversation as though our sole intention is to win others over to our point of view. Well, if that is the case, then OK. But I bet if we were to ask, people would most often say they would rather feel heard, express themselves authentically, or have a challenging exchange of views rather than simply persuade others to their view—unless, of course, they are lawyers or radio talk-show hosts.

It is extremely important to clarify our intentions in the realm of communication. We can start with a larger intention like "I want to use effective conflict resolution skills," or "I want to be a skilled communicator." Then we can formulate more precise intentions that will help us realize our greater aim. Consider these possibilities. What would it be like to learn to stay present when a conflict arises instead of leaving the room? How would it feel to be able to listen to uncomfortable feedback without withdrawing emotionally? What would happen if you allowed a friend to express a viewpoint and really listened rather than advocating your own opinion? What if you practiced saying no without self-doubt or regret? What if you learned to laugh when your ego felt threatened in conversation? Any one of these responses is possible; we only have to conceive it to begin to realize it.

The skills in this book can help us become present to what is and grow our skills from there. For example, if someone is criticizing us, we can intend to stay present rather than react and withdraw. When we stay present, we are aligning with the way things are at that moment. Full alignment with the moment, whether pleasant or unpleasant, is the essence of our meditation practice. To communicate, problem solve, deal with conflict, and work with others, we must be present to things as they are. And we must *intend* to develop the skills that will allow us to work with old scenarios in new ways.

Play of Opposites

Clarifying our intention in communication requires a willingness to be rigorously honest with ourselves, because many times our underlying motivations don't match our conscious intent. On one level I may want communion, but I may be unable to resist my urge to dominate. Or I may think I want honesty in conversation, but feel an overpowering need to please others. I may desire rich emotional exchange, but feel compelled to avoid any intensity of feeling. I may want to express openness, but I don't really trust other people. The good news is that we can practice forming the intentions to be loving, authentic, and vigorous, and over time, these intentions can help rewire even our deeply ingrained patterns.

Anytime we create a positive intention, we also create its opposite, or we bring the opposite into awareness. So if we want to listen and be more receptive, we are going to notice how often we jump in and interrupt. If we desire to question more, we are going to notice how often we sit back and fail to be curious. When we notice the opposite arising, whether in the form of resistance or negativity, we can learn to simply acknowledge it and return to our intention.

Returning to Intention

Once our intention is firmly established, we must return to it frequently. Intention functions not only as a starting point but also as an anchor when we become confused or disoriented in our communications.

While exploring intention, a Canadian student told this story. He had taken a six-month leave from work to fulfill a dream to go to the Arctic for the summer solstice so he could see the twenty-four-hour sun.

Driving along the Dempster Highway, a long gravel road going all the way to the Arctic Ocean, I passed only a few cars that day—probably five or ten, mostly logging trucks. Soon there were no other cars. I felt remote, at the edge of the world.

As I entered a valley, the air started to fill very slowly with smoke from a forest fire. There was no way to tell the location of the fire, and suddenly, things were moving and changing fast. The farther I went, the thicker the smoke. It was a long distance back, and there was no place to get gas and no place to stay. I still did not know what direction the fire was moving. It could have been valleys away, or it could have been close. I wasn't sure. There was no radio, no news. I was driving blind.

I considered turning back, but it would be so disappointing. I had come to see the Arctic Circle and the twenty-four-hour sun. I had to figure out what to do. I felt completely alone and uncertain. My rational mind ceased to be of help any longer, so I went with my gut, but in a different way than I had ever done before. It came from intention rather than instinct. I had made the intention to see the Arctic Circle and the twenty-four-hour sun. I realized my intention was the only true guide in that moment. And so I continued on.

For the next hour the smoke did not let up, and I never saw another soul. And then, feeling more and more confidence in my intention, I relaxed. I cranked up Radiohead on my stereo and began to laugh while the lyrics, "Go to sleep, little man being erased…" blared over my speakers.

Then the smoke cleared, and I emerged from the valley onto a sunny plain. I headed straight to the marker for the Arctic Circle, and I arrived about 11:00 P.M. The sun kissed the horizon as it circled.

A Field of Intentions

With our practice of intention, it's important to look at the big picture, keeping in mind that each of us is embedded in a field of intentions. All those around us, known and unknown, have their own intentions, which may harmonize or conflict with our own. I may intend to stay married to my husband, but he may take a new lover. I may intend to advise my daughter, who drinks too much alcohol, to quit, and she may choose to ignore me. I may intend to be open to feedback, but my body has a powerful intention to protect itself against threats, and I can't overcome my defensiveness.

We are subject to relational, cultural, and evolutionary impulses that may be the same or different from ours. The people we love, the groups to which we belong, and the social systems in which we function may have different intentions and different purposes. There is so much intention that extends from reasons that are ancient and hardwired into our biology. In fact, we are part of a grand evolutionary intention playing itself out—often beyond human reason and our capacity to understand it. Our intentionality in any moment is a mix of personal, biological, evolutionary, cultural, systemic, and cosmic forces.

While we can exercise a powerful effect on the world around us, our personal needs and desires do not arise independently of conditions, and we must make peace with limits to our personal power, especially in our interactions with others. For example, I have tremendous love for the man who was my first husband. He is a genius of visual art and is the funniest person I have ever known. I would have preferred for us to remain friends after our divorce, but he is very private and keeps his social life to a minimum. So I have learned to maintain my intention to be friendly and open toward him, even though he is largely impersonal toward me.

From another point of view, *not* getting what we want may be more liberating than getting it, because it forces us to dig deeper and discover a level of intention that transcends our egocentric wishes and puts us in greater harmony with our truest nature beyond all relative goals. For me, learning to love my former husband unconditionally, in spite of his social style, is a greater and more enduring endeavor than appreciating him for being my friend.

Indeed, it is essential to form an intention to discover the deepest and most meaningful aspect of who we really are, because in time, all other motives will be irrelevant. Our pile of stuff will be gone; our friends, family, and body will also go as surely as the way of all flesh. So whether the realization of this primary intention is called enlightenment or love, God, the Tao, or Being itself, we can see the wisdom in aiming straight and finding a lasting home in this marvelous universe. All other goals, however worthy, are secondary to this.

PRACTICE

Forming Intention

1. Spend a few minutes every morning, just after meditation, clearly articulating your most meaningful intentions to yourself.
2. Reflect on a guiding intention for your lifetime, such as becoming a loving person, growing into an awake human being, or being of benefit to others.
3. Form a communication intention for the day that will contribute to the fulfillment of your lifelong intention. For example, "I will become a good listener." Ask yourself, what are some of the attributes of a good listener? For example, "emptying myself of other ideas while someone is speaking; staying present to what someone is saying, asking clarifying questions," and so on.
4. Now visualize your intention by creating a detailed image in your mind of its fulfillment. What would it look and feel like if you were able to fulfill this intention? Enjoy experiencing this image of success.
5. Now bring the intention from a future focus as in "I will become a good listener" to the present tense for the day: "I am a good listener today."

4

Attention and Awareness

A student approached the poet Ikkyu
and asked him to write the highest teaching of Zen.
Ikkyu took his brush and wrote *Attention*.
THE LITTLE ZEN COMPANION[1]

MINDFULNESS CONSTITUTES THE HEART of meditation practice
and forms the basis for sound conflict resolution skills. By cultivating
mindfulness, we learn to pay attention and open our awareness to the
reality of things in the present moment—or as we like to say, "things
as they are." Even with modest intention, we can sharpen our attentive awareness and become more connected to our environment.
Mindfulness also makes it possible to bring clarity and insight to the
world of working relationships. By paying attention, we learn to respond differently to the threats in conflict situations and create new
patterns of interaction based on curiosity and a brave heart rather
than self-protection.

Meditation trains us to see and experience reality directly and
clearly. Sitting still and quieting our minds, we drop loads of con-

ceptual barriers and begin to experience the sensory details of each moment of our lives with heightened precision: the vividness of color, the vibration of sound, the feel of myriad textures, odors and fragrances as they waft past, and an astonishing variety of tastes. Meditation empties us of our habitual patterns of mind so that we can experience each wondrous moment fully, even the moments that include challenge or difficulty.

Awareness is, by its nature, perfectly still and perfectly empty. It is often compared to a mirror, simply reflecting what arises without judgment, preference, or interference of any kind. It is the open space in which internal thoughts, feelings, and impulses, as well as all of our impressions from the outer world, occur. Awareness doesn't distinguish between inside and outside, nor does it move toward or away from anything in its field. It doesn't identify with or reject; it doesn't label things as good or bad. It simply notices what is occurring and allows it to pass away of its own accord. Unbiased and unfazed, it recognizes patterns, impermanence, and the interdependency of all things.

Unless we practice meditation, however, we may never experience awareness like this. Rather than reflecting like an empty mirror, our awareness is usually filled up with a slew of extras that filter and obscure direct perception: our perpetual likes and dislikes; our unconscious beliefs; our inherited attitudes; and the ideas, judgments, and opinions we hold dear about ourselves, others, and the world. We block the view by interpreting and judging reality stiffly, according to our preferences, our wants and needs, our hopes and fears.

Awareness doesn't have a dog in the fight, so to speak. It just says, "Here things are—just like this." Korean Zen Master Seung Sahn reiterates this core Buddhist principle by saying, "In any condition or situation, our mind is clear like space. This means it is clear like a mirror: when red comes before the mirror, there is red; when white comes, white. The clear mirror never holds anything, and it is never moved by what appears in its infinitely empty face. Then when we see, when we hear, when we smell, when we taste, when we touch, and when we think, everything-just-like-this is the truth."[2]

Attention

If awareness is an empty mirror reflecting what arises in our perceptual field, attention is our ability to focus on distinctive aspects of our experience. We have at least one true freedom: how we choose to focus our attention. In each moment, we can exercise our volition and create many more choices for ourselves. Without conscious attention, we are simply dancing around in the cage of our habitual patterns, thinking we are free.

In this moment, contemplate all the ways you can focus your attention. You can choose to listen more intently to the sounds of birds or cars outside, notice the weight and texture of the book in your hands, or feel your breath as it warms and cools the inside of your nose. You can let your eyes wander around the room, receiving shapes, lines, and colors, or feel the temperature of the air on your skin.

You can identify your own emotional state or mood. Or, as you read, you can focus on a sentence that piques your interest, as well as your own thoughts about it. You can expand or contract your awareness like a camera with multiple lenses, allowing your attention to be wide and diffuse, narrow and concentrated, or both. You can tune in to the gross dimensions of reality, including the density of your body; you can feel the subtle domains of energy and light or immerse your attention in the totality of being.

Pleasure lures our attention, often without our consent; pain insists we feel it, even as we attempt not to. Learning how to be present to conflict is similar to learning how to be present to pain. Neither one feels good (unless you have developed a taste for it), but presence isn't concerned with feeling good. It is about perceiving what Master Seung Sahn called truth. By bringing our pure, open, attentive awareness to any experience, including a conflict, we learn to be present with an unbiased mind that is neither for nor against what is happening.

It is somewhat tricky, however, to include all of our judgments, preconceptions, and emotional reactions in our unbiased awareness.

So we start practicing impartiality toward our preferences and reactions. Over time, our identification with impartiality gives us the space to react less and less. We start to see more clearly. Soon we begin to develop greater equanimity and the skillful means to deal with conflict.

In any situation, with clear vision and an even heart, we can access the innate wisdom of the moment and open ourselves to the compassion that permeates our existence. We can also become acutely aware of how quickly things change and, therefore, how precious and fleeting each situation is, even if it is a troublesome one. Attention, by its nature, adds value to experience in the same way a tended garden flourishes or a seen child grows up healthy. And when given attention, as Suzuki Roshi says, "Each of the myriad things has its merit, expressed according to function and place. The myriad things include human beings, mountains and rivers, stars and planets. Everything has its own function, virtue, or value."[3]

People and the Problem of Impartiality

When we practice sitting meditation, we are more aware. We notice ordinary things more clearly, such as when a friend cuts his hair, grows a beard, or wears new jeans. We can determine our sister's mood by the sound of her voice when she answers the phone. We can sense our partner's fatigue the moment they walk through the door, before they talk about their day. And we can feel more acutely the irritability of our boss as he strides past our desk in an impatient flurry.

I have found in my own life that it is challenging—well, almost impossible—to experience other people impartially. I can view a rainstorm or even a traffic jam impartially, but I have all kinds of biases and preconceptions about loved ones, friends, acquaintances, and strangers. I have judgments about the groups I belong to and groups I don't. I have a huge number of opinions about people who are different from me and, surprisingly, people who are like me. I have judgments about them partly because I care about them so much and I want them to be unflinchingly happy at all times, and partly because I want them to perform a part in my play, if you know what I mean. In other words, we all have agendas and scripts for each other and want people to fulfill our idea of who they should be for us, rather than taking them on their own terms.

Instead of simply being mindfully aware of others, we usually react to them. We may remark that we like that haircut, but "Damn, where'd you get those jeans?" We may sense our partner's fatigue and offer advice, a compliment, or a drink to boost their spirits. And as soon as the boss is out of sight, we may confide to our buddy the fourteen different ways we wish our boss would change.

It's not our fault. We are extremely sensitive beings with highly tuned nervous systems that pick up subtle, energetic cues and unspoken signals. In the past our survival depended on our attunement to each other and the group. Yet, at the same time, we humans were extremely dangerous to one another. My husband once shared a statistic with me that, over the course of our history, we were three times more likely to be killed by another human being than by anything else in nature. No wonder we react. We react to secure our safety with insiders, and we react to protect ourselves against danger from outsiders. When our boss hulks past us in an uptight mood, it is natural and intelligent for us to shrink out of sight because we know what that monkey is capable of.

Our capacity for equanimity, however, is compromised by our judgments and reactive patterns of right versus wrong, good versus bad, beautiful versus ugly. These judgments erect a barrier between us and our direct experience. We become like a next-door neighbor peering over the fence, speculating about what's going on in someone else's house without seeing for ourselves. When we meditate, what we notice instead is our fear of difference, our defenses, and our flurry of opinions. Meditation teaches us to suspend our judgments and to be available to what is without a barrage of mental gossip intruding upon reality itself.

If we have trouble suspending our judgments and opinions over the course of everyday life, how much more difficult is it to do when "things as they are" involve uncomfortable encounters and conflicts with other people. When our ego boundaries, our preferences, or our values bump up against those of another, the first thing we do—after we feel a flush of energy—is judge the situation, usually blaming it on the other person. When I was a mediator, I used to joke that I was waiting for the day when someone came into my office, sat down, and began by saying, "I am part of a terrible problem and wonder if you can help me out of it." Instead, 100 percent of the time, people came into my office blaming the other party.

Before we get to the difficult step of taking responsibility, we must learn to practice unbiased observation; to simply be curious about what is actually occurring outside of us and inside of us. It is like placing ourselves in the audience of the large performance hall of our life and watching a conflict unfold on stage. As the actors play their parts, we can practice remaining present with an unbiased mind and observing everything, including our emotional reactions. What a marvelous, complex, and energetic collection of characters, scenery, sound effects, and props. And we don't have to do anything about it.

An Experience of Just Paying Attention

Several years ago I participated in a weekly gathering to learn sweat lodge ceremony with about ten other people. The facilitator was skilled at teaching and leading the ceremonies, but she was weak at facilitating the group interactions—at least, from my point of view.

I felt a lot of tension within the group; people seemed to misunderstand each other frequently, and communications weren't clear. Apparently, I was unconsciously trying to help us harmonize. At a certain point, the facilitator sent me a private e-mail telling me that I was a disruption to the group. She said that while my intentions were good, she experienced me as interfering with her job, and she asked me to refrain from interacting with the other participants. I was exiled privately. She never spoke to me about it in person or in front of the group.

It was a peculiar experience, but I saw that she was right about her observation of me. I was interacting with the motive to make myself feel more comfortable. And since I was there to learn about the ceremony from her, I decided to follow her instructions and just pay attention to everything going on in the group, including my own internal responses to feeling powerless and muzzled.

What a revelation! For the next month's worth of meetings, I withdrew my meddling and watched, with awareness and neutrality, as the group decimated itself. How clarifying it was for me to calm my own interior rather than trying to save the sweat lodge that didn't need saving—and to see how frequently I interefere, imposing my values and ideas on those around me.

Conscious Choice

Engaging conflict with awareness is a powerful spiritual practice because we are confronting the protective mechanisms of our ego in the moment. Much in the same way that we have learned to countenance difficult sensations while meditating, we find that we can remain present despite all sorts of impulses to do something else. We discover that an impulse is not an imperative. We don't have to save anybody.

The same is true of our threat responses in daily life. We feel like slapping somebody, but we don't slap them. We feel like helping, but we don't help. We feel like fleeing, but we don't flee. We can trust ourselves to experience the most primitive sensations of fear, hope, and aggression without doing something primitive.

By cultivating our attention and awareness, we start to reprogram the most reactive, habitual patterns in our evolutionary hard drive. When the amygdala reacts and the sympathetic nervous system shoots danger signals throughout the body, the prefrontal cortex can slow down, disengage, and watch. Like an air traffic controller, we take a breath and say to ourselves, "Gently now, gently." This command activates the parasympathetic nervous system, slowing the heart and lowering blood pressure.

Guiding this action is consciousness—the ability to take a perspective on our momentary perspective. Soon we start to relate with others not only with more neutrality but with more spaciousness. We discover the supreme power of choice. This is a big deal.

Everything changes in our lives from this moment on. When we see that we can consciously choose new ways to relate with ourselves and others, there is a ripple effect. Whole families start relating differently, office norms change, and culture has an opportunity to absorb these innovations and further them. It is not simply our personal practice; we are participating in the evolution of human consciousness. Just perhaps not in the sweat lodge.

PRACTICE

Attention and Awareness

1. For three minutes, move around and notice what arises in your sensual field. What sights, sounds, smells, physical sensations, and emotions register in your awareness?
2. Notice your biases. Do you pay more attention to the interior than the exterior or the other way around? Do you have a tendency to notice one sense to the exclusion of others? Do you turn your attention toward that which is pleasurable and away from what you don't like?
3. Open your awareness to include all of your sense perceptions equally, your exterior as well as your interior experience. Experience awareness itself as ultimately unbiased.

PRACTICE

Reflecting on Misinterpretation

1. Recall a recent instance when you interpreted something only to discover later that your interpretation was incorrect.
2. Recollect the thoughts that created the original interpretation. How did these thoughts influence your emotions and interaction in the moment?
3. Replay the experience without the interpretation. How does that alter your experience?

5

Scary, yet Exciting

Whatever arises in the confused mind is regarded as the path.
Everything is workable.

CHÖGYAM TRUNGPA RINPOCHE[1]

FOR MOST OF US, the shift away from viewing conflict as wrong
or bad is challenging. We view conflict as dangerous because it is. It
is likely that someone will get hurt; if not physically, then emotionally, politically, monetarily—you name it. Humans have a long track
record of hurting each other, that's for sure. We are always aware of
the risk. And since we don't want or need the trouble, we commonly
avoid conflict, ignore it, or walk away. Some of us are more prone to
please or capitulate to others when differences arise; others pretend
like nothing happened. Others of us have a competitive or aggressive
nature, so we might respond with anger or a secret campaign to out-
maneuver our opponents.

It makes sense that we react in the ways we do. We have a powerful
built-in defense system; our body reacts immediately and unequivo-
cally to anything that threatens us. The alarm bells deep within our

brain, the amygdalae, trigger our sympathetic nervous system and drive a cascade of physiological responses designed to protect us. Our heart rate increases, our digestion stops, our breath becomes shallow and rapid, and our higher thinking functions shut down, equipping us to flee, fight, or freeze in a matter of seconds. To move toward the conflict is counterintuitive to every fiber of our being.

As humans, we've evolved from a relentless struggle for daily survival against wild animals and hostile bands to a seemingly safe physical existence. The threats we face today are more often emotional, social, or political. But they are threats, nonetheless, because they challenge our deepest sense of safety—our belief systems, our self-image, and our ideas of right and wrong. Often, conflicts offend our views about how things should be and, even more, how people should be.

On an emotional level, conflicts can feel no less threatening than wild animals or aggressive humans. Something as ordinary as a disagreement with your mother about the holidays or a neighbor's complaint about your dog can set off the same bodily reactions your ancestors relied on in the savanna to keep them alive. Being criticized by your boss looks ordinary from the outside, but on the inside, it feels as though your life is at stake. This is even more true if you have a history of conflict or trauma, because the reactive patterns are stored in the body.

In the context of conflict resolution practice, the moments in which our ego is offended are golden. They provide the perfect opportunity to see our self-protective mechanisms at work and learn to unwind them. We can start to be curious about how it all works. We can see the role of our negative thought patterns and how they might feed a conflict. We can tap into the actual taste of our feeling states and learn to transform our emotions without suppressing them. We can take responsibility for ourselves and suspend the usual blaming and finger-pointing.

The first and best place to explore is the most dominant of our hardwired emotional responses—fear.

Encountering Fear

Conflicts trigger primitive survival mechanisms; when fear arises, the triggers take on a scary quality. Something we value is threatened; someone we know could get hurt. To a large degree, our fear is instinctual—a combination of pure bodily response and 200,000-year-old mental habits. Fear is a form of intelligence. It tells us to protect ourselves.

If we can learn to relate with fear directly—not trying to get rid of it but becoming aware of what it looks like, tastes like, and feels like in our mind and body—we can develop fearlessness. Fearlessness is necessary to working with conflict, and it comes from *including fear, not from being free of it.* The first step is to look directly at what we are afraid of when a conflict comes up. This is to admit our fear, to allow it space in our body and mind. The following are some of the fears we might acknowledge.

Threats to Our Bodies and Physical Safety. We can experience a primal fear of physical attack. This is especially true of men who have grown up with the reality that if they are not careful, they can be hit by other men. Women also fear physical attack due to our smaller size. Even if there is no literal possibility of being kicked, slapped, or roughed up, we will still pull away from potential conflict out of an instinctive impulse for physical safety.

Threats to Our Relationships. Often, we shy away or avoid conflict because we are afraid of hurting the other person and damaging our relationship. We are afraid we might do or say something that we can't take back. Our relationships are so valuable and, to some degree, fragile that we protect ourselves and each other, dealing with conflict in every way except directly. Most of us have limited experience with positive outcomes, so we won't take the risk. Even those of us who are prone to fight don't find conflicts very productive. So we try to let sleeping dogs lie—and rightly so. We are afraid we will be hurt if we engage directly.

Threats to Our Sense of Belonging. We often experience conflicts in groups we belong to, whether it is family, friends, or colleagues. We fear that by asserting our individuality or a difference of perspective, we may be judged, rejected, or ostracized. As social animals, we have a primordial need to belong, and there are few things worth risking exile for. Through most of our evolutionary history, the tribe or clan ensured our survival, and we know this instinctively. Consequently, we experience a deep fear of losing our place in the group.

Threats to Our Identity or Ego. Conflict disturbs our self-image. It brings up aspects of ourselves we don't like. We don't like confusion or overwhelming emotion. We don't like to be blamed or proved wrong. We don't like to feel stupid or taken advantage of. We don't want to be humiliated or embarrassed. And we especially don't want to feel vulnerable or exposed. Is it any wonder we shy away? Conflicts have a way of rearranging our ego and our sense of self. We are justifiably afraid of this.

Threats to What We Value. In many of our conflicts, we're trying to protect what we value—from our material possessions to our ideas and beliefs about the world. We find ourselves in conflicts over objective values like money, property, or territory. But we are every bit as frightened when our subjective values are threatened. As many wars have been fought over ideology and religion as over gold and water. Friends have fallen out over differences of opinion, as well as breaches of contract. These are often the instances in which our attempts to avoid conflict fail, and we end up in painful, protracted disputes, such as lawsuits or longstanding border skirmishes. No wonder we are afraid.

Unknown Fear. Sometimes we don't quite know what we're afraid of. We have a general sense of uneasiness, but we can't locate the cause. We literally don't know what the true source of the fear is. The experience is vague, generalized, and uncomfortable. When we look closely, we may discover that we are afraid to feel the fear itself.

Our most common reaction to the felt experience of fear is to want to make it go away. We often drown it out by creating some other, more familiar state of mind. We mute it by distracting ourselves with the Internet, picking up the phone, or going shopping. We may douse the feelings with alcohol, drugs, food, or sex. Or we may have more positive ways of coping, such as going to the office or the gym.

In the course of spiritual practice, we hope to get beyond intense feeling states like fear, aggression, pride, lust, and jealousy. But these emotional states are powerful sources of information and of life force and energy. When worked with and transformed, they bring clarity and authenticity to our experience and deep humanness to our life. Emotions make us more whole, more human, and ultimately, they inform our compassion and our awakened heart.

Energy and Intensity

When we feel threatened, the bodily sensations are certainly intense but also *exciting*. In other words, our nervous system and all other bodily systems are activated, and energy courses through us. Just think about how energizing it is when a fight or an argument breaks out. There is a moment of satori. Our attention is heightened, our senses open up, and we focus with remarkable precision on the here and now. Our eyes, ears, and mind are alert and fully present to what is happening. We may not think of it this way, but conflict wakes us up, even as we prepare to run away.

Learning to stay present with intensity, rather than shutting down or reacting defensively, is difficult because it is like hearing the sound of a crying baby. Everything in us is designed to make it stop. So the challenge is to slow down, give the feelings space, stay present, and feel the upsurge of energy in our body. We may also have to acknowledge discomfort in the gut, trembling in the solar plexus, or the confusing experience of wanting to cry. Our mind is usually flooded with negative thoughts and blame about what happened, so it is important to suspend the story forming in our mind and just let ourselves feel.

As Trungpa Rinpoche points out, "Transmutation of emotion is not a matter of rejecting the basic qualities of the emotion . . . you experience the emotional upheaval as it is."[2] We can add an even, gentle breath to our situation, which will help us manage the overwhelming sensations of the experience. As soon as the feeling state becomes manageable, however, our thoughts will usually reassert the negative story. It is important to nip this in the bud and bring our focus back to the feelings, the energy, and the wisdom.

At age forty, I remarried. My new husband was a widower and the father of three daughters, ages nine, thirteen, and sixteen. Like most people who blend families, though, I found that living together was far more challenging than I had expected. Prior to getting married, I had lived alone with just my son. I was used to quiet and order and to things being done my way. A household full of teenage girls was complicated, and the onslaught of energy, activity, responsibility, and chaos left me feeling completely overwhelmed and, you might even say, panicked. In no time, I went from a happy bride to the quintessential stepmother—the one we all know from the fairy tales, the witch, the nag, the big bad stepmom—and it was only getting worse.

Within a short period of time, I either had to get out or go in—one or the other. I decided to go in. I knew that for my own sanity, and for the well-being of our new family, I had to work with myself differently. I had never before been challenged with so much emotional intensity in my body. In desperation, I resorted to what I had learned as a student in my early twenties at Naropa Institute in Colorado.

For several months, whenever I started to feel emotionally overwhelmed, I went upstairs and sat in one particular chair. For several minutes, I suspended the story about what was happening, then felt the feeling states 100 percent: terror, claustrophobia, chaos, anger. There was an intense surge of energy in my body, and it was important to recognize the discomfort. Allowing myself to really feel the flood of those emotions helped me create the space to accept their presence. After experiencing the bodily sensations, I practiced recognizing and including their wisdom. This was the key to changing the pattern.

When I respected the message of the feeling states, I could work with them. I couldn't work with them if I just felt them; I couldn't work with them if I just gave them space. It was only by respecting their intelligence that I could begin to navigate through them. The emotions were communicating truths: the environment was overwhelming; I needed more order, more routine. After I allowed the energy to surge and then listened to the wisdom beneath the surge, I could communicate my perceptions to my husband and stepchildren in a way they could hear and then communicate my wants, preferences, and needs. And I had much more space and compassion to listen to their needs and to realize that they were also experiencing a difficult transition. That was how I was able to stop losing my temper and freaking out all the time. The methods I had learned at Naropa to transform emotions were priceless.

PRACTICE

Working with Strong Feelings

1. The next time you find yourself in a negative emotional state, take time to explore it.
2. Suspend the story about what happened, giving your attention directly to the feelings themselves.
3. Explore the sensations. Where are they located? What are their texture and tone? How are they changing?
4. Most important, feel the surge of energy as it courses through you, including anything chaotic or unpleasant in your body.

5. Breathe evenly and gently to help maintain your attention and keep your brain from shutting down.

6. What information are the feelings conveying to you? For example, a strong dose of anger may alert you to an issue you really care about or a boundary that has been crossed.

7. Return to your story, but this time accept the information and wisdom while relinquishing blame.

8. See if you can include the wisdom you received in your communications with others.

6

Three Conflict Styles

I thoroughly disapprove of duels. If a man should challenge me,
I would take him kindly and forgivingly by the hand
and lead him to a quiet place and kill him.

MARK TWAIN[1]

ONCE MY MOTHER SAID in a sardonic mood that she was going
to engrave the following words on my father's headstone: "He did
not respond." She had the consistently maddening experience of trying to engage him in their challenges, feeling she was blown off or
ignored, and then getting really mad at him. It was a predictable
pattern, and it happened all the time. My father was a genius in his
ability to ignore her.

He, on the other hand, had a different viewpoint. I'm not sure
what his viewpoint was, because in keeping with his brilliance, he
never felt the necessity to explain it. But I am pretty sure that he felt
my mother's anger was both unpleasant and unnecessary. There was
never a sense from my father that anything was worth getting upset
about, which, of course, upset my mother even more. Sometimes he

was right; other times, it would have been better for everyone if he had dealt with a problem head-on.

In meditation training, we refer to the three poisons of ignorance, passion, and aggression. These are the three basic ways we protect ourselves when faced with challenges from reality, most often in the form of other people. In the first instance, we move away and disappear (my father's style); in the second, we move toward the challenge and cling; and in the third, we move against it.

Ignorance implies that we simply ignore disturbances, much like a cow absorbed in chewing its cud ignores cars passing by on the road. When more pressure is put on us to show up and relate, we become increasingly stubborn, stolid, and unwilling to move. Soon we behave like any animal does when it hunkers down on its hind legs in order not to be led or pushed anywhere.

In contrast, the passionate style reaches out to the world, constantly grasping, acquiring, and holding on for dear life. This is a particularly human tendency, leading us to manipulate and cling to others in order to get what we want. It is as though we lived in Hollywood, attending one cocktail party after another. We look glamorous while chatting up and seducing people, but at the same time, we are always glancing around for someone or something more, different, or better. Acquisition is of enormous value to us; then we hoard our things, including our relationships.

The third style, aggression, is much more claustrophobic, irritating, and warlike. We draw boundaries around ourselves, pushing away anything that encroaches on us. This pushing away can range from a merely uptight attitude, which keeps others at arm's length, or it can become steadily angrier and more bitter. It intensifies into harping on and on about the world and the people in it, until finally, we find ourselves living and acting in a hell realm full of hatred and rage.

When I imagine the three poisons, I see a scene in which reality throws a difficulty our way. But before we deal with it, we pull over to a roadside bar to order a drink. On the menu are three drinks called I Know Nothing; Needy Clinging; and Piss Off. These are the three basic ways of responding to our conflicts. Since we rely consistently on our favorite poison to defend our ego against threats, some of us become sentimental, sloppy drunks; others become clumsy, stupid drunks; and the rest of us are just plain mean drunks who are thrown out of the bar at the end of the night.

Occasionally, we knock back one of the poisons to take the edge off; other times, we stir two of them together; and occasionally, we indulge in a combination of all three at once. When we finally get back on the road, we are so wasted that we shouldn't be behind the wheel. In other words, our experience of reality has become so distorted that we create more difficulty, confusion, and danger for ourselves and others. There comes a point when even we know we need rehab. Meditation is it.

Avoidance

Interestingly, these same three patterns are outlined in conflict resolution literature. In the Thomas-Kilmann conflict inventory,[2] *avoidance* is another word for ignorance. Avoidance simply means our impulse to withdraw, walk away, or disappear rather than face a conflict. In the extreme, this style includes the friend who zones out instead of talking over a problem, the wife who ignores her husband's chronic infidelities at the expense of her health, and the parent who fails to notice when his teenager has started using drugs again.

Maybe you have worked with someone who possesses an almost magical power of disappearing when a conflict comes up, even when they are still sitting right at the table. Or maybe you know a person who never quite understands what you mean when you try to address an issue with them. My son sometimes relies on the avoidance or ignorance strategy, only instead of disappearing, he aligns himself deeply with gravity and becomes heavier and heavier in the face of challenge, like the animal who won't be led away. Sometimes his stubbornness is so effective that it would take earth-moving equipment to get him to do something he would rather avoid.

There is a wisdom in the old adages about "letting sleeping dogs lie" or not "stirring the pot." Sometimes issues don't concern us, and we should just steer clear. Other times, conflicts will simply dissipate on their own if we allow them to. Often, walking away from a conflict or avoiding a negative encounter is skillful; sometimes it is shrewd, and occasionally it is downright scrappy.

But a habitual strategy of avoidance comes at a great cost to us. It can make us feel lonely or invisible. We withdraw our energy just when a relationship is getting interesting and tell ourselves it never would have worked out. When a new challenge comes up at work, we fail to make a contribution for fear of pushback on our ideas and then wonder why we aren't valued more. We allow problems that could have been handled easily to grow out of proportion, until our only option is to walk away. Most important, we expend valuable energy on suppressing awareness of the conflict when we could have used that same energy to solve the problem. Suppression leads to depression, isolation, and feelings of helplessness.

The reasons for our withdrawal may be good ones. We don't want to hurt other people, and we don't want to be hurt. We are afraid of what might happen to a relationship if we express our true opinion. We don't want to get mired down in situations that never come to creative resolution, and we don't want to waste our time and precious energy. We often find ourselves saying, "It's just not worth it." But habitual conflict avoidance takes a toll on our self-esteem, effectiveness, and relationships. The biggest problem with this style is that we are unlikely to even notice that we are practicing avoidance or that there are negative consequences to this strategy

Accommodation

In the conflict resolution world, the passionate style is translated as accommodation. Those of us with this style are prone to be cooperative and attentive, but when push comes to shove, we have a hard time valuing our own point of view and standing up for ourselves and our ideas. We are hesitant to separate from others, so we err on the side of staying connected, diffusing tension, and keeping others happy. Our intention is to preserve relationships, so we defer routinely to the preferences of others. We are often obsequious, pleasing, or even submissive, with the predictable outcome that, in private, we often feel like the proverbial doormat.

The accommodating type would rather be liked than thought of as difficult, would rather appear attractive than look disturbed, and would prefer to acquiesce rather than squabble. These friends are often a little too nice, call too often, and apologize unnecessarily. And even though women may struggle more often with this style, there are plenty of men who feel they are submissive in some of their relationships, often with their wives.

In a work setting, being agreeable is an excellent trait. Responding promptly and positively to a superior's requests, helping to implement others' initiatives, taking direction when it is given, and listening to the opinions of others are effective and necessary skills.

As far as our personal lives are concerned, we all enjoy the company of someone who looks out for us, who is flexible and willing to adapt, and who privileges the well-being of others, creating a positive and flowing atmosphere. Indeed, in the context of spiritual practice, these are the jewels of generosity and care.

But when we become stuck in this pattern, we run some of the same risks as the person with the avoidance style. We can lose a sense of our own self-worth, believing that our value comes from taking care of other people. Depression and helplessness often overcome those of us who accommodate too frequently, as we relinquish our own passions in support of someone else. We may feel resentful when our contribution fails to be acknowledged or someone else receives credit for the work we do. While we are pleasant to work with, we can lose credibility with our friends and colleagues because we won't risk giving our opinions or standing up for our views.

True relationship occasionally requires moments of strength, autonomy, and the courage to disagree. People sense inner strength and respect it. If someone can't say what they truly think or believe, you can't trust them, because at some point, their suppressed feelings will surface as hostility, sabotage, or retaliation.

Unlike the avoider, our compulsion to hold on keeps us in dysfunctional relationships at home or at work far longer than is healthy because we find it so difficult to walk away. Another dilemma for the accommodator occurs when there are too many people to please; differences between people and their agendas leave us wobbly, unsure of who to support. Conversely, when an opportunity to lead arises, we may fail to step up to the responsibility because we are accustomed to a support role.

In a class I was teaching on conflict resolution, more than half of my students viewed themselves as overly accommodating. They felt they were often inauthentic, even cowardly, in their communications. They regretted their inability to speak their own truth and wished they had learned the skills for expressing themselves more fully and authentically.

This is hard to imagine with so much emphasis these days on the individual and so much insistence on "being yourself," yet these students still felt unable to manifest their unique viewpoint. When we explored why they shied away from opportunities to be more direct and more real, they simply felt that they lacked the skills to ensure a positive outcome. "It isn't worth it" was a common lament.

Competition

The competitive or aggressive style includes those of us whose first instinctive response to a challenge is to push back. When the ego is confronted, competitors don't walk away, don't try to please; they respond by asserting themselves. The competitor is always up for a fight, even a friendly one, and isn't the least apologetic about their will to dominate.

In this style, conflicts are simply opportunities to prevail. Though we might relent in the short run, we still look down the road for a win later on. If aggression is our primary trait, we may be attracted to conflict and thrive on it as a way to express a fundamental attitude of hostility toward the world.

There is such a thing as healthy assertiveness, aggression, and competition. Assertiveness is catalyzing, life-giving, and energizing. It gives us the boost to express ourselves and the courage to try out our ideas and take risks in the world. It is necessary for leadership and essential for drawing boundaries in relationships, for setting limits in our life, and for preserving a sense of our own integrity. We have to be able to say no and mean it and not predicate all of life's important decisions on whether others will be happy with us or not. In one sense, our ability to assert ourselves is the source of our integrity and vitality.

Aggression in its purest form is simply our raw life force pushing outward in order to protect or prevail. Many people, men and women alike, thrive on the challenge, emotional intensity, and pressure of high-level engagement in athletics, business, law, or the media. Competition at this level is an opportunity to express ourselves more fully, to push beyond boundaries and limits, and to experience the high of working with people in highly purposeful environments with strong goals and strategies and with sustained focus and energy. A great deal gets done, and we experience a sublime pleasure. When worked with consciously, this energy can bring out the best in us.

Highly competitive people don't seem to get depressed, but they are often disliked by others. Steve Jobs was known to be difficult to work for because he was so driven and critical. Because he was such a perfectionist, however, he got the performance, products, and satisfaction he demanded. He built one of the world's most successful companies, employing thousands of people and creating beautiful instruments for the rest of us to use.

Habitual aggression, however, is the most destructive strategy for protecting our ego and securing our place in the world. If you avoid conflict, people won't notice you. If you accommodate by habit, you will still be thought of as a nice person. But overt aggression as a conflict style wears everyone down over time.

Those of us with an aggressive style put everyone else in a state of unease. The people we interact with are on the lookout for trouble, walking on eggshells, talking in low tones behind our back. We are cut off from true communication because our colleagues and loved ones and acquaintances won't risk the arguments; we end up believing we have more support from others than we genuinely do. When we experience a loss, everyone is secretly glad.

Aggression always creates a sense of separation, and we suffer from our own angry outbursts and lack of kindness. You could say we have post-traumatic stress disorder of the soul. Our relentless competitiveness gets old; we can't relax and enjoy ourselves, and when the competition is finished, we find ourselves alone, hardened, and isolated.

Always a Mix

Although one style of dealing with conflict may dominate, most of us have a unique combination of responses that is complex and varied and depends on many factors. In one mood, we may be accommodating; in the next, competitive and challenging. In one relationship, we may talk over every inch of a problem when it comes up; in another, we may never mention it. We may be tolerant with our children when grappling over an issue but tough with our colleagues. After a long day of competing at work, we may feel extremely sensitive once we are home and have little patience for conflict with an intimate partner.

Context makes a difference, as do roles. If I am a lawyer, everyone assumes I aim to win, and if I am a nurse, helpful accommodation is the order of the day. An aggressive stewardess will be fired, and an avoidant stock trader won't last long in the business. Bureaucrats learn avoidance, salespeople develop seduction, and law enforcement requires aggression. In some contexts, we develop a passive-aggressive style for dealing with each other—a mixture of avoidance and aggression. We may have learned this style from our family. As adults, when conflict is not dealt with skillfully at work or at home, we inadvertently recapitulate it, holding our power indirectly and asserting ourselves in sneaky ways—all while looking like we aren't.

Conflict styles vary widely from culture to culture. Some cultures are more direct in their communications, while in others, directly addressing an issue is considered crude and lacking in subtlety. Conflicts are navigated implicitly in some cultures, handled behind the scenes through friends, associates, and elders in order to save face; in others, conflicts are dealt with explicitly or out in the open. Some cultures are verbally expressive; jousting and arguing in front of others is a source of energy and vitality, interrupting is acceptable, and raising your voice is part of belonging. For others, displays of emotional intensity are signs of a breakdown of relationship.

When Poison Becomes Medicine

Temperament, conditioning, roles, context, relationship, culture—all of these things inform how we respond to conflict. So why is it, then, that we tend to have one predictable style? All humans are creatures of habit. We respond habitually mainly because we have never questioned the efficacy of our conflict style, nor have we considered whether our ego is really in need of all this protection.

While the three poisons—passion, aggression, and ignorance—are an instinctive response to fear, threat, and uncertainty, paradoxically, these unexamined patterns actually support our suffering by creating a deeper sense of separation and loneliness. Even the accommodating style is motivated by a lack of confidence; we feel insufficient when we're not placating others. This is why meditation practice is the basis for reliable conflict resolution skills. We need to discover our truly indestructible nature so we can let down our guard, expose our vulnerability, and step into new ways of being. Nothing short of a recognition of our essential nature will do, because the small separate self will always need to protect itself.

We don't need to change our fundamental conflict style; rather, we just need to become conscious of it. When we see our own reflexive style clearly, we simultaneously become aware of the styles of our friends, colleagues, and groups. We begin to take an interest in what else might be possible; defending our ego becomes far less interesting than working creatively with the challenges that arise.

Every poison in the right amount becomes medicine, and any medicine in the wrong amount becomes poison. While there is a negative side to each conflict style, there is positive potential when our response is based on a clear and direct relationship to the situation at hand, a confidence in ourselves beyond ego, and a willingness to make mistakes rather than a knee-jerk reaction that protects the ego and minimizes vulnerability.

Alchemy

When the energy of ignorance is liberated from the ego in need of protection, we can let things go, feel spacious, and accept how things are. We do not sweat the small stuff or fight losing battles. No longer concerned with self-protection, we can stay present instead of disappearing. This profound presence to what is frees us of our need to change or manipulate anything. There is nothing to fix.

The wisdom of passion manifests as engagement without egoistic clinging. When we free ourselves of the anxiety of trying to secure happiness through acquiring people and things, we let go and become truly generous and giving, without needing anything in return. We are open to others despite differences, and we create beauty and intimacy in our relationships.

The wisdom of aggression is penetrating clarity and power. We are self-possessed and trustworthy; we know what we think and feel, and we communicate that clearly. We are capable of asserting our preferences, but without the need to dominate or prevail. When we transform the energy of aggression, we bring integrity, rigor, and discipline to the resolution of our disputes.

With practice, we relax in all conflict-filled situations, even if getting away happens to be the skillful response in that moment. We approach conflicts with curiosity, patience, and confidence in creative possibility. We choose, according to the circumstance, when to walk away, when to let sleeping dogs lie, when to smooth ruffled feathers, and when to give a hefty push on a system that is languishing.

We value peace and equanimity in our lives. These are beautiful qualities, and meditation, exercise, and other practices help us cultivate these virtues. But the peace we experience is a result of being present to how things really are and working with that, trying to impose a serene state on our direct experience.

PRACTICE

Working with Conflict Styles

1. Contemplate a repeat conflict in your life. What is your dominant style for dealing with this conflict? Explore the corresponding wisdom of this style. With this information, how might you respond instead?

2. Perhaps the conflict is with your boss. How might you communicate your feelings with respectful clarity? Under what circumstances would it be wisest to let go of the situation, maybe even leave your job? Finally, how might you negotiate with your boss to do the work that he requires while also getting the personal time and recognition you need?

3. To cap off the exercise, consider the ways in which *all three* energies could weave into a situation and play an important role in revealing its deeper wisdom. How could this wisdom evolve the whole situation? How could it improve the relationship? How could you harness the energy in the system to fuel the needed change?

4. You can also practice balancing things out. If you tend toward aggression, you can take up the practice of listening. If you tend toward avoidance, you can try to stay present. If you are too accommodating, you can keep taking the risk of expressing your opinion until you become good at it.

7

The Marvel of Multiple Perspectives

Learn to see, and then you'll know there is no end
to the new worlds of our vision.
CARLOS CASTANEDA[1]

HAVE YOU EVER THOUGHT about what a miracle it is that we can change our perspective at will? Think of how remarkable it is to walk into an art gallery and look at a landscape painting. First, we can enjoy the realistic depiction of a scene in nature. As we lean in closer, we can then see a set of brushstrokes, color choices, and the aesthetic decisions of the painter. Stepping back and looking at the same painting again, we might see a trend in the history of art, how landscape painting as a form has developed and changed. Or we might see a valuable object that sells for a lot of money in the market. All of these perspectives arise from gazing at one work of art.

The same capacity for taking multiple perspectives is true in our relationships with other people and the world at large. We have the ability to listen, empathize with, or learn from the people around us. Just being able to nod our head at a friend and say, "I understand how you feel," is so extraordinary that we don't notice what a miracle it is. We have this amazing ability to shift our attention to experience the perspectives of others and, therefore, to access multiple realities.

Sometimes our perspective changes in an instant. An astronaut sees the Earth for the first time in space, and it is never the same earth again. A person has a near-death experience, and life after that is more precious than ever before. Sometimes we meet a person whose very being changes the way we see things. I met Ken Wilber in 2004. Ken is one of today's great thinkers, and the author of *No Boundary* and more than thirty other books about spirituality, philosophy, and science. Encountering him changed my perspective and my life. I had read several of his books during my spiritual search, but he was too smart and too philosophically dense for me to make much headway through his prose, even though I could see how important his writing is to our time.

When I met him, my first thought was not, *He's profound;* it was, *He is handsome.* And I liked how he dressed, particularly his shoes and his metrosexual jackets. And he enjoyed himself when he spoke; his eyes communicated his pleasure in language. He laughed at his own jokes, gesticulating with his pen and adjusting the legal pad on his lap—the creative tools of a philosopher. As he talked, his theory came to life, and I enjoyed listening to him. When he entered the domain of spirituality and meditation, I could feel the expansiveness of his mind beyond the concepts he was articulating, as he was always simultaneously evoking the vast space of meditative realization.

Ken implored us to remember that every story is inevitably embedded within a particular perspective. He would constantly remind us that no perspective is 100 percent true and that no perspective, however alien to our own worldview, is completely false. He would say, "Every perspective is true *and* partial. Everyone has a piece of the truth.

"At the same time," he added, "some perspectives are definitely more true than others, but there is no final and ultimate capital-T 'Truth.'" Rather, there are different kinds of perspectives, each embodying a different kind of truth with different claims to legitimacy and power. When we tell our stories, we tend to speak from one or another of these perspectives, and the effects can differ, depending on which perspective we take. As we grow in consciousness, we can inhabit more and more perspectives.

Perspectives in Conflict Resolution

When I was a mediator, I made a naive assumption about people's capacities to take perspectives. I assumed that anyone wanting to resolve a dispute in mediation would be able to see things from a point of view other than their own. I soon discovered that it wasn't that easy.

I started to see that a small percentage of people couldn't take their own perspective—literally. They were incapable of expressing their preferences, their wants, and their needs. Perhaps they had never been asked to express themselves and simply didn't know how. Some people didn't know what their wants and needs actually were. Others had grown up in abusive environments and were too threatened to express themselves. Some belonged to a culture in which the opinion of authority prevailed.

In a mediation case involving a Latino organization, I worked with a young man and his elders. He seemed thoughtful, and I felt that he had something important to say, but he never spoke. Instead, he deferred to the older men, even when I looked to him to share his side of the story. His silence communicated a steady respect for his elders, so in this context, his silence had more priority than his opinions.

Many times, I worked with people with a history of abuse who faced the same limitation, though for very different reasons. They had been so emotionally and/or physically dominated, they felt unsafe expressing an opinion. In domestic abuse cases, many victims would not speak up for fear of angering their spouse in the course of a negotiation.

Most of the people I worked with could speak on their own behalf but were unable to see the validity of the other side. I think we can all relate to that. Even though parties agreed to a solution to a dispute, they often did so grudgingly and left the session feeling as though someone had forced them to settle, because they still believed they were right about everything.

Other people were more flexible. They could see their own point of view and the perspective of the other side, but they could not entertain the third-person perspective of the law, a judge, or a custody evaluator. Still other people were great with facts or objective data but tended to get stuck there, ignoring the importance of feelings, intuition, cultural factors, and other subjective realities.

Then there was the rare person who was so fluid in their capacity to take perspectives that they could express their point of view, genuinely listen to an opposing one, and include the implications of the law and the interests of third parties in the negotiation. They were willing to feel emotions and consider subjective interests such as pride or saving face while maintaining a vigorous view about money and value. They were capable of evaluating the situation from the past and contemplating changes in the future. They could keep a perspective on the negotiation process itself and even content themselves with periods of not knowing what was going to happen.

These people were a pleasure to work with because the struggle of dispute resolution became a creative challenge of multiple possibilities. They thought outside the box, they dreamed of ways of adding value, and they imagined solutions that would be good for everyone. They, like all human beings, occasionally got stuck in their own positions, but they were consistently generous in what they offered in a negotiation, as opposed to the ones who held on to money, property, and even their children, as if their very lives were at stake.

It wasn't necessarily that the creative ones were smarter, wealthier, or even more educated. Rather, they seemed deeply at home in themselves and were less afraid of conflict than the others. They seemed to trust the creative process and were energized by the possibility of influencing an outcome that benefited all parties.

During my work as a mediator, another scenario also prompted me to think in terms of the ability to take perspectives. While I was the director of the Office of Alternative Dispute Resolution for the Utah court system, I facilitated a series of difficult, emotionally charged conversations about race, religion, and environmental issues. It was a time when people were trying to have these challenging conversations in hopes of creating fair-minded initiatives in Utah like the Task Force on Racial and Ethnic Fairness in the Legal System.

In large meeting rooms in different places around town, we would have tough conversations about race relations, ethnic bias, and institutional racism. There would sometimes be from one hundred to several hundred interested, caring people present with a dizzying array of viewpoints. Some worked for the judiciary, some for law enforcement, some in criminal justice. Others were public representatives, government officials, or social advocates from not-for-profits. Some were simply socially minded citizens.

Among these groups were people who referred to themselves as "color-blind." They believed that racial bias didn't exist anymore. They wanted everyone else to stop stirring the pot, because for them, race was no longer a problem. Other people in these conversations were pissed off, outraged, and emotionally intense. They often attacked others and demanded a reaction to what they saw as the extreme injustice in the system. Yet another group, who had witnessed or experienced the injustice, had found their own internal means for coming to terms with things and wished others would do the same. Then there were the sad, depressed, hopeless ones who didn't believe in the possibility of a fairer and more just society. They were present because they were required to be and had little to say in these conversations.

Finally, there were the rare and very valuable people who could participate in all of these points of view. They could access denial, anger, sadness, and frustration and include them all without getting stuck or burned out. They seemed experienced, compassionate, patient, and determined to make a contribution. And they were, most often, practical in their suggestions for changing the system.

I admired these people who, like some of my clients in mediation, could move fluidly through many perspectives. They were the ones who valued feelings and intuition as much as data and empirical evidence; they were thoughtful and imaginative but also practical. They appreciated the value of money but were not greedy or overly concerned with the dollars. They cared about maintaining a positive emotional quality in the room; they understood that the meeting was part of a precious day in their lives and that how they conducted themselves mattered.

I appreciated these people who were so aware, flexible, and caring and who were self-possessed even as they adapted. They were open to solutions and unattached to outcomes. These people had done their work; they had learned through experience, education, upbringing, or even karma how to see an issue from many different angles, even when they might have a very personal interest in the outcome.

After putting in some serious time in these trenches, I realized that the ability to take multiple perspectives is by no means a given; it is a developmental capacity that must be consciously cultivated. In other words, we grow into it through practice. It takes intention, awareness, emotional maturity, and fearlessness to navigate between many different points of view.

One of the challenging aspects of this practice is that, in the beginning, inhabiting multiple perspectives is stressful. Each time we embody a new perspective, we add complexity, ambiguity, and room for doubt. Coming to decisions takes longer, and we become aware that even a satisfactory decision is likely to have a downside. Rather than cope with this anxiety and doubt, we are tempted to go back to collapsing reality into a single point of view.

The good news is that in meditation we learn to hold a big

enough space for multiple perspectives. Then we can bring that open space to other parts of our lives. When we also learn communication skills, these multiple perspectives come to life.

Three Primordial Perspectives

After I met Ken Wilber, I learned what Integral Theory has to say about perspectives. Of all of the perspectives we can take, noticing three can prove invaluable.

These are the three different fundamental perspectives we take in our thinking, speaking, and writing. These correspond to the pronouns we use in everyday language.[2]

The first-person, or "I," perspective expresses my personal viewpoint, or subjective reality. It includes my feelings, beliefs, perceptions, emotions, value judgments, personal history, memories, and other aspects of any story that is unique to me.

The second-person, or "You," perspective encompasses our shared viewpoint, or intersubjective reality. It includes our shared stories, cultural values, social agreements, common language, and the various ways we mutually resonate at a subtle or emotional level. A second-person "We" perspective might contain the shared history of a relationship between two people, or it could embody the unconscious cultural beliefs held in common by millions.

The third-person, or "It," perspective points to the empirical viewpoint, or objective reality. It includes facts, evidence, proof, data, science, and legal findings, even the perspective of outside observers —that is, how "he" or "she" or "they" view the situation (or are affected by it).

As we participate in conversation, talk over our differences, or enter negotiations, these three perspectives are always at play. It is important that we learn to use them more consciously, because as we will see, each one reveals a different dimension of reality and therefore discloses a different truth.

PRACTICE

Taking Perspectives

1. Consider a time in your life when your perspective changed. It may have been a small shift like seeing yourself in a photo and deciding to lose weight. Or it could have been a large shift like suddenly seeing that the world is a benevolent place.
2. How did you see the situation in the beginning?
3. What caused your viewpoint to change?
4. How do you see the situation now?
5. Can you find a point of view that includes both ways of seeing?

8

Three Perspectives, Three Truths

There are three sides to every story: yours, mine, and the truth.

UNKNOWN

CONFLICTS HAVE A WAY of provoking our interest in truth. Whenever my son, Willie, has a conflict with someone—most often with my twenty-year-old niece, Rachel, who cares for him twice a week—I get a phone call. He usually begins by describing the situation.

"Diane," he says, "Rachel is giving me a hard time again. She says I am not coming outside to the car soon enough, Diane. But it is not me, Diane; it is Rachel. She is always giving me a hard time, Diane. That's the twuth. That is the twuth, Diane. OK. Good-bye." These phone calls always end with the assertion, "That is the twuth." He instinctively knows that calling on the "twuth" will convince me that he is not to blame for the conflict. She is.

Indeed, it is natural for all of us to look to "twuth" when we want to be exonerated, vindicated, or simply supported in our perspective. Setting aside notions of absolute Truth (leaving that to the philosophers, scientists, and Zen masters for now), what are we looking for when we reach out for "the truth"? Something reliable, something real. Is Willie a laggard, or is Rachel impatient? Which is true?

The truth reveals what is. We depend on it as a source of strength and clarity and as a basis for integrity. It is something we should easily agree about. But, like Willie, we have a tendency to conflate "the truth" with "my twuth." Therefore, trying to persuade others of "the truth" usually means trying to win them over to our way of seeing things.

Of the many insights of Integral Theory, one that I have found particularly useful in the context of conflict resolution work is the distinction between first-, second-, and third-person perspectives and the kind of truth each reflects. These are the perspectives that we use every day in our speech and writing and that correspond to the pronouns "I," "You," and "It."

These perspectives are so near to us that we don't see them. But when we look closely, we see that each one expresses a different facet of truth. The first-person dimension, "I," is personal and subjective truth; the second-person "You" becomes "We" as it illuminates the truths between us—our shared values and beliefs; and the third-person "It" conveys the tangible truths of the objective world.

Learning how to differentiate and acknowledge each one, and then including all three, gives us a much fuller picture of what is, and ideally, what could be. Utilizing multiple truths in this way is sometimes referred to as "taking an Integral perspective."

First-Person Perspective

The first-person, or "I," perspective expresses my feelings, beliefs, perceptions, and values—or for that matter, any view of things as I see or experience them. This perspective is unique to me and obviously subjective. In conversation, we refer to this perspective as "my" truth. It is what Willie sees and complains about in his conflict with Rachel. At the same time, it is also what Rachel experiences when she arrives to pick up Willie, and he won't come to the car.

Each of us operates from the uniqueness and limitations of our first-person point of view. It is our existential predicament to interpret reality through our own private lens; but this lens is shaped by beliefs, conditioning, and social contexts. While we can lean over and look for a moment through each other's eyes or walk a mile in each other's Nikes, when it comes down to it, as the B-52s say, we are each living in our "own private Idaho."

The first-person perspective can be thought of as an internal Thoreau's cabin in the woods that provides sanctuary, free from the pressure of social approval or empirical tests. We don't have to prove anything to ourselves. Here, in our private retreat, we can make our own observations and draw our own conclusions; we can think our own thoughts, sort through our deepest dilemmas, and make peace with ourselves. Or not. This privacy can be a source of great freedom, or it can turn into a prison of our own making. The first is the experience of self-realization, while the second is the predicament of the curmudgeon.

Whether great or small, spacious or limited, the first-person perspective is real. Even when limited, distorted, demented, screwed up, perverse, or failing to correspond to anyone else's reality, as a perspective, first person just is. To that extent, it is true.

We might protest that "sometimes people are just wrong," and their perspectives should therefore be ignored. But they can't be. A first-person perspective that is out of sync with society is a first-person perspective that is out of sync with the "We." A first-person perspective that strays from objective fact is a first-person perspective in error. But it still has validity within itself.

When I was a psychology student, I learned how important it is to honor the first-person perspective. We often worked with psychotic clients who were exiled from society because they could barely participate in consensus reality. I learned that if I was going to work with these clients, I needed to grant them their experience, however deluded, at least as a starting point. If a client said, "There are voices coming out of the television," I learned it wasn't my job to talk them out of it. I could simply listen and then invite them to eat supper, straighten their closet, or take a walk outside to relieve the electronic assaults.

This training taught me to respect my clients deeply and to strive to see the sanity within their highly exclusive perspective. By acknowledging the first-person perspective, I could work with anyone, because there was enough dignity and respect to form a relationship. Indeed, this training made a deep and lasting impression on me; it changed my perspective on all of my relationships.

A friend of mine, who is a public defender, has a similar orientation. Appointed by the state to defend those who can't afford a lawyer, she works only on appeals, taking cases to the higher court after her clients have been convicted at trial as a possible result of procedural errors or some other injustice in the process.

She rarely wins an appeal. Furthermore, the clients she represents are often difficult, with extensive criminal records or a mental illness. They will lie to her; refuse to cooperate or to take responsibility for their situation.

Even so, she maintains an abiding respect for them, trudging up to the Utah Supreme Court, briefcase in tow, again and again on their behalf. It isn't that she is a bleeding heart. She is a tough, seasoned public defender, who manages to keep her mind and heart open against the odds. I admire her diligence, her commitment to fair representation, and her capacity to see into the inherent dignity of her clients, in spite of the corrosion in some of their characters.

The willingness to identify fully with first-person perspective is essential to the work of artists and poets, masterful psychologists, and (as in my friend's case) advocates. Whether invoked from deep inside ourselves or accessed by truly listening to someone else's perspective, the purpose of first-person perspective is not to establish absolute Truth. Rather, it is to access an entirely unique view of the world.

Usually we can accept our own first-person perspective or that of the people we admire or love. But it can be challenging to acknowledge the legitimacy of *all* first-person perspectives. The very thought of it makes us uneasy. How can we grant legitimacy to a perspective that asserts homosexuals should be exiled from society or a young woman should be stoned to death for a sexual experience? The answer is to learn to make a hard and fast distinction between acknowledging the existence of a perspective and agreeing with or condoning it. We often refuse to listen to a perspective for fear it will be interpreted as agreement.

For example, if my partner or spouse tells me that he is worried about whether we will have enough money in the bank to cover our expenses in the coming month, I can hear his concern without necessarily agreeing with him. I may have a different perspective about how dire our financial situation is. I can acknowledge his perspective, or I can agree with it. Keep in mind that *acknowledgment does not equal agreement.* When we make this distinction, genuinely listening to another's point of view becomes more possible.

Another common confusion is when we conflate third-person truths with first-person opinions. If my partner insists, "I am freaked out about money," while hollering at me in the kitchen with a bill in in his hand, that is a very different statement from "We don't have enough money," or "There is not enough money in the bank."

Notice the use of the tense. "I am freaked out" begins with "I," which indicates it is a relative statement about his mind state, while "We don't have enough" implies that I agree or should agree. The statement "There is not enough money" shifts the focus to an objective statement of fact, so we might have to solicit the expert opinion of a financial manager. Simply using the first-person pronoun "I" frees us from the argument and allows us to freely exchange perspectives.

In the context of conflict resolution, granting the validity of another's first-person perspective is key. It magically opens the door to problem solving because all people—including you and I—become more agreeable and more relaxed when our point of view is, at the very least, acknowledged. Offering respect is an act of good faith that can be felt; like a cold beer on a hot summer day, it has an immediately soothing effect.

When we are in the thick of our disagreements, it can be a relief to remind ourselves that each of us relies on our first-person perspective to navigate the terrain of reality. Sometimes for better and sometimes for worse. Either way, we are each entitled to the dignity of our first-person perspective.

Third-Person Perspective

The third-person truth, or "It" perspective, indicates reality as it is viewed from an objective distance. Sometimes that distance is unimaginably large, such as the space between a telescope and a planet, and sometimes it is inconceivably small, such as the space between a microscope and a cell nucleus. The third-person perspective requires the space between the observing subject and the observed object to be preserved. That distance is central to the scientific method, central to the position of neutrality, and is what we mean by *objectivity*.

Third person is the realm of "it" or "its," of "this" or "that." These pronouns are objects and are further away from reality than "I" or "You." In conflict resolution, third person is the perspective that we conventionally think of as the objective truth. It includes facts, evidence, proof, data, scientific and legal findings, and instruments, such as recording devices and video cameras. It also includes the perspectives of ideally unbiased, outside observers, such as judges, witnesses, and referees.

The third-person perspective is the great domain of science and empiricism. Recently, I was arguing with a friend over whether there is such a thing as a true third-person perspective or if there are only interpretations, and before I knew it, she had gone to Wikipedia to look up the definition of empiricism. Inadvertently, she "proved" the point I had been making: that we consistently reach for objective reference points to verify our perceptions of the world.

In the research lab, we require a hypothesis to be verified repeatedly by other researchers before we accept the results as true. In our court system, we strive for objectivity by attempting to eliminate subjective influences that could be biased, unwieldy, and unpredictable. We look to evidence, to law and precedent, and to facts. The catch, however, is that in the court system and even in the research lab, information is always interpreted and contextualized by human subjectivity.

Nonetheless, the third-person perspective is concerned with reliability and predictability. Consider for a moment how dependable the great third-person art form engineering is. The third-person truths that have emerged in math, physics, and chemistry have helped us to construct an astounding environment with everything from skyscrapers (which emerged from Elisha Otis's invention of safety brakes for elevators) to spacecraft and satellites. We have incredible mobility due to the innovations of automobiles, bridges, highways, railway systems, airplanes, airports, and electronic communication systems. Barring design or mechanical errors or metal fatigue, these structures hold up amazingly well.

We can fly across the ocean to another continent in less than eight hours. Can you imagine? One comedian jokes that every time we are on an airplane we should be holding on to our seats and squealing like children. Indeed, over the last few hundred years, all kinds of technology have poured forth from the third-person perspective, changing our lifestyles and transforming the world in which we live. Amazing. And there is no end in sight. Yet the third-person perspective still fails to settle our disputes for us.

Honestly, you would think that it could. You would think that laying out some hard facts would put some conflicts to rest in the same way that looking up a word in the dictionary settles our disagreement over its meaning or finding a date in Wikipedia establishes when Bob Dylan released his first album. In these simple scenarios, produce a fact, and poof! Disagreement disappears.

But if you have ever been to court, you know that when a judge or jury makes a determination of law and a finding of facts, one side still goes away unhappy. Sometimes both sides do. As Voltaire said, "I was never ruined but twice; once when I won a lawsuit and once when I lost one." Rather than accepting rulings from a court, we prefer to cling to our own versions of truth. Rarely, in my experience, does a third-person perspective alone resolve a dispute—unless both parties allow it to happen.

Second-Person Perspective

Enter the second-person, or "You," perspective. The second-person truth exists in relationship between "I" and "You" in the domain of "We." These are the truths that exist between us: our shared beliefs, our cultural values, our agreements and commitments, as well as our ethics, empathy, compassion, and mutual respect.

Ken Wilber often refers to the second-person dimension as the "Miracle of We," because it is totally miraculous that we humans have the capacity to be so cooperative. Almost no other species outdoes us when it comes to communicating, organizing, and agreeing about things, except maybe bees and ants. We are ridiculously social, and we get along with each other far more often than we don't. The truths of the second person are the invisible ties that bind us, keep us lined up and flying gracefully forward like geese in a V formation.

Conflict resolution and mediation are ultimately second-person enterprises. To bring people together "into one mind," we must weave first-person perspectives together with helpful third-person information and data, such as business or home appraisals, neutral evaluations, profit and loss statements, or photographs of damage to a car or apartment. And then we must agree.

Once a divorced couple came to me with an issue regarding their son. They had gotten along well after their separation, but now that their son was entering high school, they had run into a serious conflict that was costing them their peace.

They could not agree about where to send him to school. The father insisted that it was time for the boy to grow up and be challenged, and to that end, he wanted to send him to a large high school known for its academic rigor. The mother believed in the importance of relationship and individual attention, and she wanted to keep their son in the same small, private school he had attended for the previous six years.

My first step as the mediator was to acknowledge the validity of each of their first-person perspectives. Rigor and relationship: I could find room for both. The next step, however, was to do some third-person research. Could they investigate schools that might fulfill both of these criteria? In no time at all, they had come up with a third alternative that satisfied them both, as well as their son. Problem solved.

This is a very simple example that demonstrates how, with respect for each subjective opinion, we can research objective solutions and come to an agreement. This solution was far more durable and satisfying for them as a family than asking a court to decide the issue on behalf of one side or the other. Can you imagine if we had argued over which was more valuable, relationship or rigor? Or put the son in the middle of the conflict between his parents? By casting a large net over all three perspectives, we caught possibilities that didn't exist before.

As we talk through our differences, negotiate, and come to agreements, these three perspectives are always at play. All three arise and evolve together. One is not more true than the others. Each one reveals a different dimension of reality, and when we take them as a whole, we have access to a much bigger view of reality.

But in emotionally charged conflicts, the challenge lies in holding a big enough space to accommodate all three perspectives. When we are upset, we immediately assert our point of view, narrow our vision, and start talking about our old friend, the "twuth." There's no problem with that, Willie, as long as you include Rachel's "twuth" and have a clear agreement about what time you said you would come outside and get in the car.

PRACTICE

Three Perspectives, Three Truths

1. Consider a current conflict or disagreement.
2. Find a friend to listen to you as you explore the three different truths of the conflict.
3. Begin with first person, and describe your version of events in detail. Experience this way of telling the story as completely true and legitimate.
4. Now tell the story from the first-person perspective of the other player in your conflict. Do your best to enter their world, to see the circumstances through their eyes.
5. Bring an objective perspective to bear. How does the situation look to a neutral witness or bystander? Is there any relevant, objective information that might be helpful? Is there a neutral observer, someone who could offer a third-person perspective on the situation? Can you include that information as a more objective viewpoint?
6. Finally, look for the overlap between your version of the story, the other side's, and the neutral perspective. Can you find a perspective in which everyone can agree? How does it feel to settle into the shared point of view of "We"?

9

Speak for Yourself: The Importance of the First-Person Perspective

You might as well be yourself,
everyone else is already taken.
OSCAR WILDE

"I." CONSIDER HOW MANY TIMES a day we use this word: I have thoughts; I have feelings; and I have a body, preferences, dreams, desires, and disappointments. I am happy, then I am sad. I am flattered or offended, forgiving or vengeful. I am hard at work, late for an appointment, or stuck in traffic. I am happy to be home, fatigued, or ready to party. Sometimes I am sick, sometimes wrong. I am alone or busy with people, overwhelmed by things and all the stuff I have to do. Sometimes I don't even know who I am. But I love this word *I*, and I want to express it.

"I" is, of course, our most familiar perspective, the lens through which we receive and interpret most of life's experiences. "I" is so close to us that, mostly, we don't even see it as a perspective. We take it for granted that it is reality, which means we may assume it is our only reality.

But when we look closely at this "I," it can be hard to pin down. It is not exactly our body since we can lose a limb and still be ourselves. It is not exactly our thoughts because, Lord knows, they change as often as our feelings do. If this "I" were based on our memories, our sense of self would be as sketchy as an old photo album. Given the number of people who come and go in our lives, our self-identity doesn't depend solely on family or relationships. And while culture gives us clues as to who we are, we are grateful not to be what we see on TV. Or perhaps we wish we were on TV. Then there is the fact that we will die.

There are many moments during the day when this "I" miraculously disappears. When we focus on work so rigorously that we lose track of ourselves or are so compelled by the beauty of nature that our humanness ceases to matter for a time, or when we consider the well-being of our child so thoroughly that our own needs disappear, we glimpse reality without the intervention of the "I" filter. Every night when we fall into a deep sleep, the "I" reference point vanishes as surely as the Earth turns away from the sun. Upon waking, we sometimes have to work to put the self back in place.

The self is neither solid nor fixed. Further, we see that when awareness is focused on something larger than the small self—a goal, beauty, or a desire to help others—our mood is happier and our energy freer. We feel less demanding, emotionally cramped, and frustrated. Indeed, all spiritual traditions remind us in their own way to seek a life beyond the self-centered perspective, to serve others, and to recognize all of reality as our True Self.

Self-Development

From the point of view of developmental psychology, growing an individual identity is a critical step in human development. Paradoxically, we can't grow beyond the limits of our small ego until it is well established. First we need to learn how to care for ourselves and be responsible for our own lives. Only then do we have the capacity to reach beyond ourselves to others and to the world.

But this notion of a True Self can raise perplexing questions at first. One of my students, who is in her early twenties, started running marathons to strengthen her ego and self-esteem. The discipline invigorated and empowered her, and it supported her growth in all areas of life, including her meditation practice. Then she became confused when she encountered the famous saying of Zen Master Dogen, who wrote, "To study the self is to forget the self."

She had just begun to establish firm ego boundaries, to say no, and to experience a healthy sense of self-esteem. So it was disorienting when she heard that she was supposed to, as she surmised, go back to putting others' wants and needs ahead of her own. There appeared to be a contradiction between her psychological well-being and her spiritual search. Indeed, as we practice meditation in a Western context, our culture's focus on healthy self-esteem seems to conflict with Zen's emphasis on forgetting the self.

On the one hand, we grow up with the advice "Be yourself." We are encouraged to value freedom and individualism, and we are almost expected to do our own thing. We are told to be authentic, seek self-fulfillment, and develop self-respect. In school, we are challenged to do our own thinking, prompted to raise our hand and to give our opinion, and to be clear about what we stand for. We are taught not only that each of us is entitled to our perspective but that we should express it.

And then we start to practice meditation or other forms of spiritual practice, and the self suddenly becomes something to get rid of. "To study the self is to forget the self." My Zen teacher, Genpo

Roshi, used to talk about the powerful Japanese masters who would walk through the *zendo* carrying the Zen stick and shouting to the students, "Die on your cushion!" Zen practice is not concerned with improving the condition of the small self. In fact, it isn't concerned with self-esteem at all.

Ken Wilber wrote his first book, *Spectrum of Consciousness,* in response to his own inquiry into this question. He wondered about the relationship between the many approaches to psychological well-being and the different descriptions of spiritual awakening. For example, in one tradition, enlightenment refers to the direct recognition of unqualified awareness, empty of solidity and substance, immeasurable and ungraspable. In another tradition, enlightenment is considered a boundless field of unconditional love. Some mystics define enlightenment as the full, unitive experience with All That Is. Still others describe a deep communion with divine intelligence. For some, it is best described as empty; for others, as consciousness itself. Most wisdom lineages transition to using poetry to describe it, then give up language altogether, pointing instead to our direct experience.

How enlightenment occurs varies from person to person. Some people are enlightened spontaneously; others, after years of diligent effort. Some receive it as a blessing from a guru, while for others it falls into their lap as a mysterious gesture of grace. Through his writing, Ken did pioneering work in mapping out this territory. (For a complete discussion, see Ken Wilber, *A Theory of Everything.*[1])

Among other contributions to our understanding of enlightenment, Ken approached the question from a developmental framework. In this context, enlightenment can be understood to be an evolutionary process in which awareness unfolds into greater and greater identification with reality. In other words, the sense of "I" continues to expand its capacity, embracing more and more, moving beyond limited egoistic concerns until the self becomes the Self and includes everything that arises within awareness—all aspects of our experience from our own body and mind to children, families, communities, nations, all of humanity, the great Earth and her life forms, ecosystems, and eventually, all form and space in the vast cosmos. Form is emptiness, emptiness is form, and nothing is left out of the experience of what is "me."

In this framework, enlightenment is not a binary proposition: "I am enlightened," or "I am not enlightened." Rather, like nested Russian dolls, it is an elegant set of unfolding perceptions. As development continues, we relinquish attachment to identity altogether.

In ancient China, when Emperor Wu asked Bodhidharma, "Who are you?" Bodhidharma replied, "I know not." He answered this way, not because he didn't know his own name, but because his True Identity couldn't be captured by it. This is the case at higher and higher levels of development. Experience is appreciated, loved, and allowed to come and go as lightly as a dream appears and vanishes upon awakening; a dream that, interestingly enough, is suffused with love.

Including the Ego

Although the developmental point of view does not see the small self as an inherent problem, it acknowledges its limits; the small self suffers from the problems of separation and competition, and it is subject to evolutionary imperatives such as the struggle for survival and the fear of death. Because of its wants, needs, and preferences, this small "I" is an extremely narrow lens through which to view reality. It can't help but experience the stress of constant striving to protect itself and fulfill its own desires, while ruminating about how things should be different than they are.

There comes a moment in our development, perhaps born of this suffering, when we learn that we can step outside of our ego's functioning and observe it at work. When we "disidentify," or step away, from the ego and watch it instead, this is the beginning of "waking up," a defining moment in our development. In time, we learn to let go of our attachments and rest naturally in wakeful awareness while the demands of the ego come and go.

When we pay attention, we see that the ego, no matter how healthy and functional, is prone to the suffering of separating from the rest of reality. We see our compulsion to be greedy, to desire more from experience, always grasping at new shoes, cars, lovers, or insights. Or we succumb to cravings and impulses that eventually turn into addictions. We also see that we can free ourselves from these compulsions.

We see the similar but opposite tendency of aversion, to push away situations we dislike or people who trouble us. We write people off or give them an internal "f— you." This tendency leads to perpetual conflict and violence in our life. After we have pushed others away, we beat ourselves up, judging ourselves as right then wrong, fearing our mistakes while asserting our superiority, all the time needing, like a small child, to be recognized and heard. In the realm of the ego, it's a rough neighborhood.

With practice, it becomes easier and easier to recognize the destructive patterns of ego and to replace those tendencies with more basic kindness and positive regard. This kind attention enables us to develop healthy egoistic structures. We learn how to extend compassion and loving-kindness toward ourselves and our suffering. We learn to see that the "I" perspective is always limited and sometimes blind. That is its nature.

Nevertheless, it is also innately worthy. Like all things in this great mystery, the small self is worthy of the compassion that shines on all beings. By being kind to ourselves, we can access greater awareness and perspective. My student's meditation practice is supported by her marathons, and her growing self-confidence creates a strong container for her to recognize the pristine awareness beyond it. Compassion becomes our natural attitude, informed by kind moves and skillful actions. Rather than fighting the ego off, we accept it so fully that it becomes like a quiet child sitting in the lap of awareness.

Finally, the most powerful and liberating use of the first person comes when we use it to take responsibility for ourselves and our actions, particularly when they injure or distress others.

We can say something like "I am sorry," or "I made a mistake." Like the quick turn of a valve on a sprinkling system, a buildup of tension and energy is immediately released, and the relationship is refreshed like a lawn on a hot summer day.

A simple statement like "I am confused" will paradoxically sometimes set a conversation straight. "I don't know" almost always opens up a wide space for questions and inquiry. There is a power to expressing vulnerability from first person, but only a very few of us know how to do it consciously without crossing over into self-pity.

Using the first person to be accountable for ourselves, we discover this equation: Responsibility creates freedom and freedom creates responsibility. We soon learn to express ourselves with more openness because we see that we are as free to speak our minds and hearts as we are willing to be responsible for what we say. Therein lies the true magic of first person.

Speaking as "I"

In a conflict resolution context, it is imperative to recognize the legitimacy and dignity of our small "I." In fact, the ability to speak from a clear first-person perspective is a sign of healthy integration of the ego. A healthy ego is one that can express its desires, wants, and needs, negotiating on their behalf, while at the same time recognizing that many other perspectives also have validity. A healthy ego can remain light and fluid about the outcome.

Expressing a first-person perspective is a remarkable privilege of existence. Some people have never had the opportunity to speak their mind freely. Perhaps they came from a household or a culture that only allowed the views of an authority figure, a fundamentalist religious perspective, or a repressive political agenda to be expressed. Many people in the world live in a culture that prohibits speaking your mind, even among friends.

When I was young, I didn't understand why the teachers in my school put so much emphasis on freedom of expression, but as I have grown older, I see their point. The freedom to express our personal opinions and feelings in a supportive, even protective, environment is a rare condition we can easily take for granted. Like the analogy of a fish to water—we are so at home in it that we fail to feel how wet it is.

The Reluctance to Speak in First Person

There is an art to expressing a valid, healthy, first-person perspective. To cultivate the art implies that we need to practice it. We encounter many obstacles to speaking our perspective with energy, clarity, and warmth, and we have good reasons for holding back:

> "I have a fear of harming the relationship."
> "I'm worried about what others will think."
> "When I express myself openly, I make myself vulnerable to other people's judgments."
> "What if I'm wrong?"
> "I worry that I won't be understood or that I'll be misinterpreted."
> "I will be seen as self-centered."

I recently facilitated a group of powerful CEOs in a learning process. We were exploring how the three different perspectives of "I," "You," and "It" informed their decision making in their companies. I asked them which of the three perspectives they preferred to speak from. Not one person in a room of two hundred claimed to prefer the first-person perspective. Keep in mind, these are leaders of companies, and I know that good leaders have very powerful first-person perspectives. Their vision, passion, and confidence inspire others to follow them.

But we are subject to the crazy-making norm that not only are we supposed to become wildly successful, we must behave as though we have no self-interest at all. Acknowledging the first-person perspective means we're self-centered or arrogant, so we behave as though we should only think about what is best for others at all times.

Indeed, acknowledging the first person *to the exclusion of all other perspectives* is self-centered or arrogant. But when we speak consciously from the first-person perspective, we are being honest and awake, and we are owning our self-motivations. This is why I am much more relaxed around people who consciously acknowledge their self-interest than with those who pretend they don't have it.

"When it comes to giving my opinion, I feel it's not really entirely my opinion. It is more like a collection of things I read or ideas that I have about things. What do I really know?" Our opinions are informed by everything in our experience, including conversations, reading, television, films, and travel. Our opinions are always influenced by the people and information we have been exposed to. To offer our opinion is to understand that it is limited, and we aren't mixing up or conflating our first-person perspective with the third-person perspective. When we speak in third person, we actually lose authority because it sounds like we are claiming the truth for all time and all people. The local, subjective "I" is more compelling, because it is based on our own unique perceptions. The trick is simply not to confuse a first-person perspective with a third-person truth. If you are speaking a third-person truth, you need an objective reference point. That is all.

The beauty of first person is that when we consciously express it, no one can disagree with how we see things; we are not claiming the truth for anyone but ourselves. Although the "I" perspective is informed by relationships, information, and other experiences, it still comes from the integrity of our unique perceptions. To say, "I love the color blue," is a very different statement from, "Blue is the most beautiful color." "I believe this candidate is the most qualified for the office," is not the same as saying, "She is clearly the best person for the job." In first person, we are not required to cite evidence or expert testimony. We are simply saying, "This is true for me," and no one can argue with that.

A clear first-person perspective offers us a kind of sovereignty. In other words, it is the one place in language where we have a place to stand in our own truth. It isn't *the* Truth of third person, which needs empirical backup. It isn't the shared truth of second person, which requires us to agree about what is true. It is simply *my* truth. Our first-person perspective can never be appropriated by anyone, and therefore, it can be a source of dignity and strength.

"I want to express myself because if I don't, I feel isolated afterward; I feel disconnected, like I don't belong." Our opinions are not only valuable but necessary for experiencing the fullness of our being. We are expressive creatures, designed to communicate in a variety of modes. Just as a wave is an energetic expression of the ocean and a flower is a glamorous expression of a plant, each of us has particular qualities that are unique to us. They naturally blossom through words, music, bodily expression, and what we make with our hands. Each of us is imbued with innate intelligence, wisdom, and we want to offer it. We want to be seen. If we don't risk expressing ourselves, something irreplaceable will be missing from the whole.

Martha Graham, the great American choreographer, has been quoted as saying, "There is a vitality, a life force, a quickening that is translated through you into action, and there is only one of you in all time. This expression is unique, and if you block it, it will never exist through any other medium and be lost. The world will not have it. It is not your business to determine how good it is nor how it compares with other expression. It is your business to keep it yours clearly and directly, to keep the channel open."[2]

First-Person Perspective Choreography

When we awaken to the genuine validity of the first-person perspective and genuinely commit to expressing ourselves truthfully, with feeling, honesty, and depth, we also become much more willing to listen to others when they speak their truth. Chögyam Trungpa said something that always stuck with me: "Be yourself, the world will give you feedback." And it will. If you want that feedback to work in your favor, try working with the following moves.

Use "I." When you want to share your opinion, begin your statement with "I"; for example, "I would like to talk this over," "I would like it if you would listen to me for a few minutes," or "I appreciate how kind you are to me." Beginning your sentence with "I" locates the communication in the small self, the local self. The "I statement" is empowering because it cues your listeners that you are not talking about Truth or Them with a capital T. You are expressing the inherent truth of your local perspective, as well you should.

Harmonize Body, Speech, and Mind. To be effective in our communication, we need to make sure that our body, speech, and mind are all communicating the same thing. We know what it is like when someone is sending a mixed signal our way. They may be saying yes but shaking their head. "You wanna go out?" "Sure." The mouth is willing, but the head is saying no. Someone may be yelling at you but repeating, "I'm not angry." If we want to be heard, we need to clarify our thoughts and speech and make sure our body is communicating the same message.

Include Feelings and Energy. Most of our communication is nonverbal. Our brain is organized to intuit feeling states as much as it is to listen to words. One of my students recently recalled her father's complaint that no matter what her mother said, she said it in an accusatory tone of voice with aggressive energy. In nearly every interaction with her mother, her father felt like he was being interrogated and judged, which made it very difficult to "hear" her. (She may have communicated that way because he never did listen to her.) For our communications to become more clear, we have to be aware of our feeling states and honor them.

Feeling in communication is incredibly powerful. In his "I Have a Dream" speech, Martin Luther King, Jr., communicated his passion and conviction through evocative imagery, his movements, and his voice. Years later, this speech still moves us because of the energy he conveyed and the depth of the first-person voice. With his language, he shaped a future vision, and with his heart and energy, he convinced us it was possible.

If There Is Something You Want, Ask for It.   Identifying our desires or needs enables us to ask for what we want, and our communication feels more legitimate and direct. The listener can relax because the request is on the table. The listener isn't reacting to an unspoken agenda or implicit idea that they should do something differently. A simple request means we can respond. Maybe we will say yes, maybe no. But the clarity of the request frees both of us.

In the 1960s, Marshall Rosenberg developed the process of Nonviolent Communication.[3] This process is based on the idea that all human beings have the capacity for compassion and resort to violence in speech or behavior when they don't have a way to address and satisfy unmet needs.

Nonviolent Communication proposes that if people can identify their needs, the needs of others, and the feelings surrounding those needs, harmony can be achieved. It focuses on many aspects of communication: self-empathy, listening to others, and authentic self-expression. Most important, it suggests that we make our needs transparent to ourselves first and then ask others for what we want. It is a practice in making real requests of each other. When we make real requests, we can give real responses.

PRACTICE

Speaking in First Person

1. What is it like for you to give an opinion? Complete the following sentence with whatever comes up spontaneously: "When it comes to giving my opinion, I..."

For example, "When it comes to giving my opinion, I notice I care what other people think." That might be one way you complete the sentence. Another way might be, "When it comes to giving my opinion, I feel really good about it, but sometimes I overstate it."

2. Write down all of your responses without favoring any of them.

PRACTICE

Asking for Permission

1. Sometime during the next week, when something important comes up that you want to express, ask someone to listen to you. It can be your partner, one of your children, a colleague, or a friend.

2. You can begin by saying, "I notice I have a strong opinion (or I notice this matters to me). Would you give me just two minutes and listen to what I have to say?"

3. Use first-person "I" statements. As you describe the issue, notice your feelings. Name them—all of them, the obvious and the subtle. Is there a desire underneath your feelings? Is there something that you want or need? Can you ask for it? What would you have if you got what you wanted?

   For example, I might say to my husband, "I am upset right now because you didn't tell me your sister was coming to town. I feel irritated, alienated, and powerless. I want to feel that we are in sync and that we join together to plan for our family events." Or, "I want to be able to book a motel in plenty of time, because this house isn't big enough for all of us."

10

Listening:
The Art of Second Person

I would say that what we hear is the quality of our own listening.
ROBERT FRIPP[1]

SOME YEARS AGO a close friend of mine developed a friendship with a heroin addict who lived on the street. He spent most of his adult life there, except for the seventeen-some years he was in prison for drug dealing and robbery. During their unlikely friendship, he was in and out of a drug haze, jails, and hospitals. As you might expect, I was leery of their relationship and worried about her involvement with him.

One day we were talking like girlfriends do, and I asked her, "What's with this friendship?" She replied without hesitation, "He is a profound listener." She went on to say that his natural aptitude for listening had been honed through years of attending AA and countless other rehab programs. Yes, she conceded that drugs, police, jails, hospitals, and the relentless, urban corrosion of the streets were try-ing, but when he listened, it was all worth it.

I was struck by the poignancy of her description. Two strangers from entirely different backgrounds and karmic circumstances ex-changing in a genuine give and take of experience. He loved hearing her talk about poetry, philosophy, and her persistent life questions, and she was captivated by his viewpoints that were informed by the unvarnished experience of the street.

Listening can be an entryway from one world into another. Ken Wilber refers to this as the "Miracle of We" or second person. Our perspective shifts from "I" to "You," and suddenly, we emerge into another world. When we discover our commonalities there, the gap between "I" and "You" closes, and we become "We." From then on, it is a dance of sameness and difference between us. The sameness gives us cohesion; we recognize each other and feel we belong. The differences give our relationships vitality, heft, and occasionally, as you know, good problems.

Good listening is the key to all communication. Jimi Hendrix couldn't play guitar the way he did without the genius of his listen-ing; all the great poets listen to their own voices, as well as meter and space. Gardeners listen to plants; math geniuses listen to their equa-tions; race car drivers listen to their engines; and good parents listen to their children. And, of course, listening is essential to all conflict resolution.

Listening is so powerful as to be almost alchemical in its ability to transform a conversation or conflict. When someone feels really heard, everything changes. Anxiety diminishes, defensiveness disap-pears, and true communication begins. Many great healers, includ-ing Sigmund Freud and the listening lineages he inspired in the West, have found that one of the ways to help people heal is to let them retell their story deliberately in the company of someone who is fully present and receiving it with an open, nonjudgmental ear.

One of my favorite stories about the potency of listening is re-counted by Ram Dass in his book *How Can I Help?*, which he wrote with Paul Gorman in the 1980s.[2] A Tibetan doctor to the Dalai Lama, while participating in grand rounds at either Harvard or Yale, was giving a teaching about the Tibetan system of diagnosis, which involves listening to the winds, or the pulses in the body. Another doctor, who was Western trained, obviously quite successful, and worked at an Ivy League school hospital, joined the entourage—reluctantly at first. He wasn't interested in the Tibetan doctor's perspective, but since he had made the trip, he decided to stay.

The entourage went into the room of a woman in a semiconscious state. As the Tibetan doctor approached her bed, he said nothing. He lifted her wrist and listened carefully to the pulses on one side of her body, which took him about ten minutes. Then he went around the bed and listened to the pulses on the other side of her body. Then he quietly put her hand down. As he started to leave the room, the semiconscious woman sat up in her bed and said to the doctor, "Thank you." The Western doctor was astonished. He realized that even though he had palpated a thousand pulses, he had never actually heard one.

Listening is not passive. It requires intention, openness, and generosity. When it is done well, it has great impact and can transform the outcome of a communication. That is why it is called *active listening*—because it changes things. It can shift the dynamic in emotionally charged conversations or add depth and energy to our exchange. It helps people calm down, opens up space for new possibilities, and gives the speaker the rare and valuable experience of being heard. It reminds us that we are nothing if not relational creatures with an extravagant gift for communication.

A student of mine was having a rather mundane argument with her husband. He began to get upset and started raising his voice louder and louder. She could feel her own emotions heating up, but instead of shouting back, she decided to listen for just two minutes. It was the assignment from our class that week. She simply listened and looked at him while he continued to vent. The clock ticked. Finally, he broke out of his pattern and said, "Why are you looking at me like that?" Then he started to laugh and asked her directly for an apology. She said suddenly, "I'm sorry," which surprised them both, and this time, they giggled. As my son would say, "Problem solved."

There is one catch to being a good listener, and it is a significant one. We must relinquish the "I" reference point. In other words, we have to surrender our attachment to the internal voice in our head. This is the familiar voice that, like our own personal Rush Limbaugh, rarely stops commenting. Even though it is a blowhard, this voice helps us orient ourselves in the world and remain aware of our own opinions, and make no mistake, we depend on it like talk-radio listeners depend on sound bites from their favorite station. We are very attached to the messages of this "I." It is our most reliable false reference point; we know it, we love it, and we count on it. Because it is so familiar, ever demanding our attention, it takes practice, maybe even courage, to let it go.

Letting go of this "I" is like a free fall into open space. There are no reference points to hold on to; we don't know what is coming our way. We hold no images about ourselves or who we should be, and we let go of preconceived ideas about the other person and what they are going to say. It becomes a wide-open field; a completely fresh place, where nothing is assumed or taken for granted. We reside purely in the presence of not knowing. In this regard, listening is a total letting go. Chögyam Trungpa Rinpoche is supposed to have said about our lives in general, "The bad news is that we're in a free fall. The good news is that there's no bottom."

Why We Don't Listen?

Not every communication requires full, present listening. But if it has such power to change our communications, why don't we listen this way more often? If you ask yourself that question, you might notice a flurry of answers: "I'm busy.... I'm distracted.... I don't have the energy for it.... I'm not interested.... It won't matter.... He didn't listen to me.... I'm thinking about my rebuttal.... I don't

want to give up my own opinion.... I've heard it a thousand times....
They won't tell the truth.... Because it makes me sad."

When people express pain, we often fail to hear them precisely
because it hurts. If we open up, we can't help but exchange with the
feeling sensations of pain. It registers as a contraction in our belly,
an ache in our heart, or a clenching in our throat. It is often the case
that when people first come to long meditation retreats, one of the
first emotional experiences that surfaces is grief. New students find
themselves inexplicably crying on the cushion and often can't even
say why. But in a world where everything changes, loss is intrinsic to
our experience, and our hearts are more tender than we know. Where
there is loss, there is sadness. Where there is sadness, tears. And where
there are tears, if someone else is around, there is an opportunity to
comfort and be comforted.

It is completely natural for us to comfort each other when one of
us is in pain. We start doing it when we are toddlers. One of us starts
to cry, and the other waddles over in a diaper to offer a baby hug.
Later on, this comforting of others becomes a compulsive defense,
and we use it to ward off feelings without even knowing we are doing
it. Like true grown-ups, we give immediate advice, try to fix the problem, or give a rational explanation of what worked for us in the same
situation. Sometimes we offer a nervous patting on the back like an
anxious sorority sister trying to reassure ("Everything will be OK").
Actually, the baby hug is better because it doesn't promise anything.

The key to listening to people's pain, paradoxically, is to be clear
that we are not responsible for taking it away. The entire study and
practice of Buddhadharma is designed to address the problem of
human suffering. With time, we come to understand that simply
being present to each other is our most basic moral obligation. There
may be occasions when we can lend a helping hand. There may be
instances when we are obligated to interfere, but more often than
not, simple presence provides a context for others to listen to themselves, and that is the real service. Letting go of responsibility for

other people's states of mind is fundamentally liberating. When we feel free of pressure, we are happy to listen, so we listen well. In the context of practice, releasing ourselves from this responsibility is to learn—again and yet again—what it feels like to let go.

"Because they aren't listening to themselves." In the early 1980s, I spent a month with a good friend, an artist, who lived on the Lower East Side of New York City. He was the first person I knew who had AIDS, which at the time was still a largely unknown and terrifying illness. It was obvious he was very sick, but he wasn't talking about it directly. His hair and beard had grown out, scraggly and unkempt. He wore a worn, brown bathrobe and leather sandals all day and looked like an ascetic monk from the Middle Ages. He was engrossed in a whole series of food rituals that were unlike him, but he never explained why he was doing them. I remember asking him how his health was, but he avoided answering me. It was strange—and disorienting—to be with him. I recall how upset my husband was at the time. He kept saying things like, "Why isn't he telling us? It's obvious that something is terribly wrong."

"Well," I said after thinking it over for a minute, "I don't think he's telling himself. If he's not telling himself, how can he possibly tell us?"

Even when someone isn't speaking to us directly, we can still listen. "When we truly listen to somebody," as Krishnamurti points out, "completely, attentively, then we are listening not only to the words, but also to the feeling of what is being conveyed, to the whole of it, not part of it."[3]

Without a direct conversation, I could still hear my friend's terror, his emotional distress, and his physical struggle. Even though he never spoke about it, I heard the overwhelming fear that he didn't know what to do. It was clear that we had nothing to offer him besides our presence—a kind of whole-body listening. I wasn't able to empathize fully because I had never been so ill, and at that time, the term *AIDS* hadn't made it into our vocabulary, and doctors couldn't explain his condition. While he was coping the best he could, all we could do was to be open to his unspoken pain and confusion—and therefore, our experience. There was no fixing it, and like so many others during that time, he died within a year of my visit. In the aftermath of the loss, I could say with certainty that I was there for him.

"I'm afraid of what I'm going to hear." We have the most difficulty listening when we don't want to hear what the speaker has to say. Maybe we don't respect the speaker's opinion on a matter, or they are delivering bad news about a project we are invested in. Or maybe they have a political or religious opinion that we would rather not hear. It is most challenging when they want to give us a drop of negative feedback about ourselves. Even the smallest amount of unwanted reflection pricks our nervous system, and we defend against hearing it.

If you want to feel your listening skills degrade, just ask someone to give you a piece of constructive feedback—any constructive feedback. However skillful you may be at receiving, there is still a moment when you can feel your body contract and the energetic boundaries go up, bracing against the affront to the ego. With practice, we can learn to relax our defensive reflexes, becoming available to valuable information about how others experience us.

How to Listen

So how do we become better at it? We do it by emptying our minds, just as we do in meditation practice. My favorite illustration of emptying out is this oft-quoted story about the famous Japanese Zen master Nan-in, from the Meiji era in the latter half of the 1800s.

A university professor came to him, inquiring about Zen. As Nan-in explained, the professor frequently interrupted him with remarks like, "Oh, yes, we have that too."

Finally, Nan-in stopped talking and began to serve tea. He kept pouring until the cup overflowed.

"Enough!" the professor once more interrupted. "No more can go into the cup!"

"Indeed, I see," answered Nan-in. "Like this cup, you are full of your own opinions and speculations. How can I show you Zen unless you empty your cup?"

To listen, we must intend to listen and then open, relax, and receive the words, impressions, feeling states, and energetic cues from our friends as they speak. We steady our attention, remain fully present, and allow our heart-mind to exchange without interference from our internal commentary of evaluations and judgments. We mute our "react and respond" button. We simply hear what they have to say, releasing the grip of the ego on our perceptions.

Sometimes we have a confused notion that listening means agreement. It doesn't. Whether we agree or don't is a separate matter; we need to hear what someone has to say without confusing it with whether we see things the same way. But we can extend empathy or a positive feeling of goodwill, nodding our head, showing them we are taking them in. Even if we can't fully understand, we can hear. This goes a long way in the art of being human.

When you listen with your whole being, the reference points of this and that, right and wrong, good and bad drop away, and you receive more completely what's being communicated. One of my students expressed this beautifully when she said, "I feel a lot of anxiety if I'm trying to listen from a space of language. In that realm, I'm often reactive. But when I drop deeper and receive more directly with my heart and my body, there is more information available."

Paradoxically, if we privilege language less, we seem to listen more. We hear the quality of the speaker's voice, the rhythm of their words; we notice body language. Our awareness includes details from the whole space: a cat licking her paws, the neighbors talking on the street outside, a plane buzzing overhead. Nothing is left out. The whole of experience is contained in that moment of listening. A student asked a Zen master about truth. He responded, "Can you hear the breeze in the pines?"

PRACTICE

Two Minutes of Listening

1. Next time there is a moment of tension in a communication, make an intention to simply listen for two minutes.
2. Remember the Zen master's instruction to empty out. Let your rebutting mind relax. Give up your opinions and judgments for this short time period.
3. Let the communication in, simply receiving it with your whole body. Steady your attention, stay present, and note that everything is welcome.
4. Be curious. If you like, ask a question or two to help clarify the communication. A good question might be, "What else can you tell me?"
5. Remember that listening doesn't mean agreement, so empathize if you can. Extend a feeling that the speaker's experience is valued.
6. Finally, repeat back to the speaker what you heard. Be natural, using their language and some of your own paraphrasing. Mirror the speaker's energy as accurately as you can. Withhold giving your opinion about what the speaker has expressed. Simply open to being a vessel of receptivity for a moment.

11

Witnessing: Through the Lens of Third Person

To be impartial is to be the ruler.
LAO TZU[1]

WHAT IS THE THIRD-PERSON perspective? And how does it come into play in our conflict resolution work? We remember third-person pronouns from school as *he, she,* or *it,* or in the plural *they, them,* or *those guys.* In storytelling, third-person narrators often speak through an omniscient, observing voice that remains aloof, unnamed, and uninvolved, like God if he had a pen.

It might be easier to think of the third-person perspective as the telescope through which we view the night sky, the detachment with which we study a graph, or the distance from which we watch our children play. From third person, we see our own kids as a curious observer might, not as an interested parent filled with pride or concern. We glimpse them for a moment existing wholly apart from us—unique, different, unknowable. In that rare moment, we are awed by the mystery and dignity of their autonomy.

Third person is the objective perspective, and even when viewing something extremely close-up—through a microscope, for instance—it maintains rigorous distance from the object. The purpose of this distance is to perceive objects and situations without the biases and distortions of our first- and second-person perspectives. I like to think of the third-person perspective as the position of ultimate respect. We experience an object on its own terms, wholly apart from us. We are not interfering, evaluating, or manipulating it (or him or her), yet we give it our full, unbiased attention because it is worthy of it through the sheer fact of its existence. How cool is that? I sometimes suggest to my students that they practice viewing their partner from the third-person perspective so they can discover the wonder of perceiving someone they love without the filter of their own wants and needs.

Third person is the realm of witnesses, judges, scientists, referees, and accountants. We depend on these practiced, neutral observers to assist us in numerous ways. I remember once, when I was a mediator, I worked on a gender relations problem in a courtroom with a woman judge from the court of appeals. I was all about talking to the people, listening, empathizing, and sharing different perspectives. She was all about the provisions of the law, explicit courtroom protocols, and what had actually transpired between people to cause the conflict. Together, we were a great team. She needed my heart and my interest in the interior and feeling dimension of people. I needed her objectivity, clear head, and practical good sense. Together, we succeeded in helping the five men and one woman work out their issues amicably.

Science employs the third-person perspective to establish empirical truths. That is what makes it science. In proving their hypotheses, scientists have to test their theories, reliably reproduce results, and finally, demonstrate them to other scientists. Only then can they claim something is true. In fact, from the scientific perspective, nothing is true until it is proven. Science is entirely dependent on the third-person perspective. When these truths are applied and tinkered with, we create a proliferation of technologies that serve us in all kinds of ways, including supplying us with even more information. We may use the information to our perceived benefit, but the perspective itself is empty of positive or negative values.

Science makes use of these instruments and technologies to free research from human biases and interpretations. These days, there is a massive bloom of these instruments, most notably computers. I heard recently that our technological innovations are doubling every year and a half. Can you imagine? Our reliance on instruments and machines to provide third-person, neutral perspectives is everywhere around us—from instant video replays in professional sports to fully automated airline flights to DNA evidence in courtrooms. I recently got a parking ticket for an expired registration. They had photographed my expired plate and showed it to me when I stood at the counter to pay the ticket. The photo itself didn't have an agenda, but the parking people used it to make sure I paid the fine. There is nothing quite like the objective, measurable circumstances of an overdue parking ticket or an expired driver's license to help us toe the line.

The usefulness of the third-person perspective is obvious when we're dealing with money. While money itself is supposed to be an objective measure of worth, nothing is more likely to be distorted than our financial dealings. Therefore, well-written contracts provide the basis for sound business transactions, appraisals establish fair market value, and blue books tell us what our cars should sell for.

There is a reason that conventional wisdom warns us to keep our relatives and friends out of our business deals. Mixing the two leads to cronyism, nepotism, and theft by our cousin. Ethical businesses strive to operate with transparency now, keeping their books open, sharing their profit and loss statements, and letting numbers tell their shareholders the objective story. All of this supports a measure of integrity and intelligence in our financial dealings.

Objective criteria can be extremely helpful in a conflict—that is, when we choose the third-person perspective. During the course of an argument with your partner, looking up the meaning of *obtuse* in the dictionary might settle whether your use of that word was insulting. Wikipedia will sort out whether Jimi Hendrix wrote "Hey Joe" or reworked an earlier, traditional tune. And when the stakes are really high, Apple and Samsung can call on lawyers and the courts to determine who is stealing ideas from whom.

The ideal of an independent judiciary to settle our disputes depends to a large degree on third-person principles. Just laws, neutral judges and juries, standards for empirical evidence, and impartial witnesses are attempts to create the best conditions for delivering fair results. Judges are trained to be unbiased; juries are instructed to be fair. When an eyewitness is summoned into court, he or she is imagined to be a perfectly neutral bystander, someone who by sheer fact of circumstance will report what happened without the distortion of emotions or biases. This demonstrates our faith in the third-person perspective. Our legal system is fraught with problems, but if you have ever lived in a place that doesn't have an independent forum for justice, you know how much worse it can be.

In the classic television series *Dragnet,* Joe Friday, a stony, no-bull-shit investigator for the LAPD, says the same thing in every interview with a witness to a crime or accident: "Just the facts, ma'am." This is a third-person mantra. Like *Star Trek*'s Mr. Spock, Friday is a paragon of aloof objectivity, and he asks only for the same in return. In an ironic but predictable twist, it turns out that Joe Friday never uttered that famous phrase. What he did say was, "All we want are the facts." Comedian Stan Freberg liked the sound of "Just the facts, ma'am" in his stand-up routine, and that's why we associate those words with the old TV series. Like comedians, we all tend to distort or twist the facts for our own purposes. By the way, studies testing the validity of eyewitness accounts show that they are not so reliable after all. The question then becomes whether we can trust the validity of the studies. Thus comes the perpetual collapse of postmodernism.

Postmodernists assert that it is impossible to free ourselves of first- and second-person perspectives. They say that in spite of our engineering feats, human subjectivity inevitably creates wobble. They say we can't create pure instruments that will give us all the relevant information for our inquiries; these instruments are the inventions of humans. Nor can we ask a completely objective set of questions of the instruments, because the questions themselves arise from the deep context of our human interests, attention, preferences, and needs.

The third-person perspective can provide reliable information about how to build a stable bridge or a marvelous skyscraper, but it doesn't address the fate of the human spirit. We can create telescopes, rockets, and space stations; and even though we are in awe of these innovations, the greatest symbol of third person, the Hubble telescope, won't save our souls.

Fair enough. It is not the job of this perspective to save us; in fact, the perspective itself is completely indifferent. It is the source of empirical truth; it generates mathematics, architecture, and modern medicine, along with the countless technological innovations of their application. But it is also the source of nuclear weapons and has as much destructive capacity as creative potential. Third person reveals empirical truths, but it doesn't make value judgments about how the knowledge is used. That part is always up to us.

Still, the third-person perspective opens our minds and can motivate our hearts. When people—ordinary citizens and astronauts alike—go up in space and look down on our beautiful, round, blue planet, they all report the same overwhelming experience: love. Love is the crown jewel of relationship, and sometimes distance does make the heart grow fond. Love is what Joe Friday feels after he has a drink.

Indeed, these truths all live together; all our perspectives interact: the "I" of our subjective truth, the "You" and "We" of our human interactions, and the "It" and "Its" of the objective world. Third-person truth cannot stand by itself. It isn't meant to. But it does offer a distinct perspective that conveys information and knowledge for us to work with. Third person in the form of witnessing is deeply intrinsic to our fates as humans. It won't save us, but it does inform us. We can consciously invoke third person for all kinds of good purposes, while acknowledging that our spiritual destiny remains in our own hands.

Witnessing: The Skill of Third Person

The practice of witnessing is itself a marvel. Just think of those wild descriptions of near-death experiences, as the witness hovers above the hospital bed or beside their mangled body on the road. People who have had such experiences report no emotional charge, no panic, not even fear. They watch as the drama unfolds—curious, aware, and completely safe.

Meditation is the consummate practice in witnessing. We learn to sit still and simply pay attention to what arises in our awareness, remaining entirely neutral about it. It is quite remarkable that we can observe ourselves in that way, that we can detach enough to take a perspective on our perspective. The ability to take a perspective on ourselves is the beginning of freedom.

Before meditation training, we somehow automatically believe that our thoughts, feelings, and sensations are literal; we believe that they belong to us, they *are* us, and we are therefore loyal to them. We have a kind of Stockholm syndrome of the mind, beholden to our thoughts, judgments, and feelings that, like captors, imprison us and bind us to the suffering of our small mind.

Meditation trains us to become neutral observers and good witnesses. We learn to watch without attachment, simply noting what comes and goes in our body and mind. A burst of self-recrimination arises. *Hmm.* A random erotic fantasy flows through. *OK.* Hostility erupts toward a friend. *Really?* A new and creative idea emerges. *Look at that.* A bout of pride swells. *Alrighty then.* A sore knee persists. *Whatever.*

We learn to observe them all, not reacting to them, not believing them, and not identifying with them. We simply allow them to come and allow them to go. If Joe Friday were coaching us in the practice, he'd say, "Just the thoughts, feelings, sensations, and perceptions, ma'am." He would instruct us that as witnesses to ourselves, we are not obligated to form any opinions or judgments about what comes up; we don't have to decide for or against anything. Our role is to observe innocently, noting whatever arises and watching it all change. With practice, our identification shifts from the objects of our awareness to awareness itself. Over time, the practice ripens into an attitude of equanimity toward all things as they are. We learn to see the world with the same kind of nonattachment that we have practiced on the cushion. We become freer of our biases, judgments, and preferences and more open toward the world as it is.

Sometimes simply witnessing can have a positive effect on a situation. I remember once working with an irate lawyer who was upset at a hearing. He was mad at his young male client for some unknown reason, he was mad at the client's father, he was mad at the prosecutor, and he was mad at the judge. I was there to support his client in negotiating a plea bargain, and I wasn't in any position to talk the lawyer down. I remember him striding intensely down the hallway toward me. I looked into his eyes; he glared back. I just kept looking, without any agenda or particular judgment about his mood. I didn't intend to keep looking at him, but I did. When he reached me, his entire demeanor had changed. He began speaking to his client more gently, and he started asking him careful questions. He had softened considerably. I'm not sure why. I can only say I witnessed it, but I can't explain it.

Many times in our life, a situation calls for us to be present and neutral. There is no way to help, no ability to intervene, and by default, we can choose to be present to what we see, what we feel, and even what we think without offering our opinion. On rare occasions, we might be asked for it. Rarer still, someone may listen to our neutral observations and take them to heart. Either way, there is always dignity in being present to whatever arises.

Bernie Glassman Roshi is known for his teachings on bearing witness. He has organized retreats in the streets of America's inner cities and in the former death camps of Europe. He teaches his students that we can be present to any situation no matter how troubling. Everything, he teaches, deserves our attention—the most unsavory scenes and the most heartrending circumstances. He encourages us to be present, unbiased, and available to what is without imposing preconceived ideas or judgments on our experience.

Our simple presence dignifies our life; some say it actually enhances it. We start to see that we are the eyes of the universe seeing itself, and there is a profound beauty in noticing all that is. When our witnessing is deep enough, as Roshi teaches, "There is no separation between subject and object, no space between I and thou, you and me, up and down, right and wrong."[2] The gap of the third-person perspective closes as bearing witness reveals the oneness of all life.

PRACTICE

Becoming a Witness

1. Sit quietly for five or ten minutes and simply notice your environment, the details around you. See if you can be completely unbiased toward reality, and notice the deep relaxation or sense of peace that pervades your body. When a judgment or preference arises, notice it and simply include it in your exercise of witnessing.

2. Notice your ability to see different perspectives as they arise. You can see the point of view of the small self and the perspective of others; you can experience memory or a fleeting thought about the future without dwelling on either. What is this miracle of awareness that can take a perspective on all these perspectives?

3. Take a perspective on a conflict you have been involved in. Identify first with your own point of view. Now take the view of the other. Pay attention to the capacity to shift points of view, appreciating how marvelous that is. Now imagine you

are a neutral outside observer of the conflict. This is hard to do, but try. Can you look at the conflict as an unbiased bystander might? What do you see when you choose to view the conflict from a neutral point of view? What does this observer have to say about you, about the others involved, about the situation itself?

4. Invite a friend to offer a perspective about a troubling situation of yours, something they don't have a stake in. As they give you the outsider's perspective, notice how quickly you would like to persuade them of your viewpoint. Resist the natural impulse to persuade them to see it your way. Honor their viewpoint precisely because they were willing to offer it to you.

12

Everything and Nothing

I'd like to offer something to help you,
but in the Zen School,
we don't have a single thing.
IKKYU[1]

ONCE IN A WHILE, without any effort, our thinking mind completely drops away. It could happen when we are taking a long, quiet
drive through Nevada, falling into a moment of loving another person, or just sitting deeply in meditation. It could be that we have
suffered so much over a breakup that one afternoon we finally just
drop it all—the whole catastrophe as they say—and sit quietly on the
couch, watching cars slowly pass by in the evening light. A tender
calm prevails; all struggle is gone. We aren't sure where the struggle
went, but for a change we are completely free of the compulsion to
make anyone wrong or bad. In fact, we are free of wanting to change
anything at all. Our mind is totally free. We rest in an open field of
presence. The moment is full, immediate, and strangely OK just the
way it is.

This letting go can be a momentary experience, a gradual change in perception that accrues through practice (perhaps over lifetimes), or it can be a sudden, life-changing event. In her TED talk "A Stroke of Insight," neuroscientist Jill Bolte Taylor describes such a dramatic experience caused by an aneurysm in the right hemisphere of her brain.

As the blood vessel burst and the bleeding began, Jill watched from the inside an event she had studied as a neuroscientist from the outside. She recognized that she was having a stroke, but rather than panic, she remained calm and observed as she was trained to do. She watched as her sequential, linear, cause-and-effect view of reality faded. Gradually, as she tried to dial 9-1-1, she lost her ability to talk or make sense of numbers. At the same time, she began to notice a powerful perception of wholeness that was free of time. The feeling was utterly expansive, utterly joyful. What some people experience through years of meditation was happening spontaneously as a result of an injury to her brain. It was a profound and life-changing experience. She lost all of the stressful reference points: who she was, what she wanted, and what she had to do.

Like seekers of old who were suddenly enlightened, Jill can't contain her joy when she speaks about this experience. She is inspired and funny as she brings out a real human brain for us to look at, spreading the good news that "we are all one."

How do we refer to this kind of openness, a space so large that it contains all things? In the Zen tradition it is sometimes called Big Mind. To describe this in words misses the mark, but let's just say that our perception opens to a boundless, energized space in which we feel whole and utterly complete. Everything is included: This means me, you, us, all of us, all of it. One seamless whole. This experience is what so excites Jill Bolte Taylor in her TED talk.

Eckhart Tolle calls this state of mind Presence; Ken Wilber refers to it as Ever-Present Awareness; and Byron Katie calls it Reality. Others may call it Universal Substance, perhaps even God. Whether you describe it from the inside as Awareness, or from the outside as Reality, the distinction between me and it does not exist.

The experience itself is simple yet profound. As Big Mind, we feel fully present and at home with the way things are. For real. Everything is in harmony precisely as it is, precisely because it is. Time and memory cease their constant harping on our attention; we are relaxed with no pressing agenda. Our heart tenderly opens, and kindness extends outward toward all things. Or maybe we receive the kindness that is extending toward us. It's kind of amazing.

When you think about it, awareness is amazing. It is the one constant in our life. While everything else has undergone changes—our body, our relationships, our physical surroundings, and our shifting senses of identity, in every moment since we took form, awareness has been present. From moment to moment to moment the remarkable fact of awareness endures. The more we identify with awareness itself, the more coherent our lives become.

At a certain point, we see that awareness doesn't belong to us alone but, in fact, belongs everywhere. Chögyam Trungpa gave this example: "Sitting and listening [to a lecture], you have developed or created a certain type of attitude. You are directing your attention toward the speaker; but also you know at the same time that you and the speaker are not the only people [in the room], so there is the sense that you are sitting in the middle of the inside of this space— underneath the ocean, so to speak. And awareness brings about your relating with that particular experience, which is tangible, real, experiential."[2]

Sitting meditation hones our capacity to let go of whatever arises in our living experience rather than clinging to or rejecting it. This letting go allows us to connect to this larger-than-life space. At first, we may try to rid ourselves of distracting thoughts and feelings. But over time, our identification shifts from the thoughts to the space of awareness itself. Then a steadiness appears that allows whatever comes up to come up and then to pass as it will. We learn equanimity.

So we begin by relinquishing our attachments to thoughts and forms. As the space opens up, we allow for the forms to simply be what they are. Intimacy with our experience begins to develop, because we are no longer deeply for or against the phenomena of our lives. Everything has its place—even our physical pain, confusion, negative thoughts, and fatigue. So do our comfort, clarity, optimism, and bursts of creativity and love. Again, we allow everything to come and go as it will, trusting. As Zen practitioners say, "No doubt the universe is unfolding as it should." We become friendlier and more familiar with ourselves and others while at the same time identifying less with both.

In one of Rumi's most popular poems, "The Guest House," he says that everything that arises in the mind is greeted as a gift. Everything is invited in exactly as it is: "A joy, a depression, a meanness. Some momentary awareness comes as an unexpected visitor. Welcome and entertain them all."[3] Rumi extends a beautiful invitation indeed. But it can be challenging to accept what arrives through the door of our own mind and even more challenging to invite in the perspectives of others.

Open Space

In the context of conflict resolution, the open space of Big Mind is the perfect place to allow other points of view to enter. The egoistic space is small and cramped, and as filled with likes and dislikes, preferences, and opinions as a hoarder's house is with magazines. Resolving a conflict from the egoistic perspective is like walking into a tiny upstairs apartment in the city. In the summer. There is barely enough room for one idea, let alone two. But when the boundaries of identity are thrown open like windows to the sky, there is more than enough space for other viewpoints, differences, and potential ways to solve problems. In fact, there is infinite space and time.

A truly unbiased mind is a welcome antidote to the narrowness of our conventional points of view. Willie has such a mind. One day when Willie and I were out in the garden together, I looked at the flowers and asked him, "Which is your favorite?" He paused, considered, and said, "All of them." The funny thing is he meant it.

Conflict can actually give us access to Big Mind. Perhaps we are faced with a persistent problem such as an addiction, a painful falling out with an old friend, or a business deal that has gone south. In the beginning, we probably did our best to hold on, ignore or fix the problem, or otherwise make it go away. We probably blamed someone else for the trouble, got pissed off or resentful, or conversely decided that we were the bad one, the one who had made all the mistakes. But even an apology didn't fix our situation. When a problem is a gnarly one that can't be fixed or solved easily, we have to discover a much deeper capacity to accept and work with the way things are. Meditation shows us that the vastness of our mind and heart is large enough to include anything, even our most painful conflicts.

I am deeply indebted to my Zen teacher, Genpo Roshi, for his Zen practice and his work with the facilitative process that he called "Big Mind." We met for the first time in 1993, and I began to practice seriously with him in 1998, after he married my husband and me in a Zen ceremony in Salt Lake City. He was always an impressive figure, full of intensity of purpose, life force, and vigor. When he spoke, dharma flowed in simple and passionate terms. His talks conveyed his deep commitment to practice and to the lineage he received from his Zen master, Maezumi Roshi.

I was particularly impressed by the steadiness and strength with which he showed up. In contrast to the prevailing culture of our time, when our attention can drift in a thousand ways, Roshi was unwavering in his commitment to the practice. Not only that, he held the space for others to practice with him. Rain or shine, he was there every morning at 6 A.M. He was there in the early light of summer, and he was there in the dark of winter, when the Rocky Mountain cold was a formidable obstacle for anyone who preferred rolling over in the warmth of their own bed.

On those difficult mornings, only those with the deepest faith and deepest doubt made it to the zendo to sit, and he was there for every one of us. He met with anyone who had a question. Whether they were filled with longing, curiosity, or angry projections, he shared his understanding of the dharma. Hundreds of people came to the Zen center at that time, and the depth of my teacher's generosity was moving. Like Hakuin Ekaku and the ancestors before him, Roshi maintained an unbiased, swinging door for the constant coming and going of many seekers.

Ours was a very harmonious relationship; that is, until it wasn't. I shared his intensity of purpose, his love of dharma, and I very much appreciated him as my teacher. Then one day it all changed. I suppose disagreements had been building between us, but it felt more like everything flipped overnight. I could no longer see things the way he did, and it was very disorienting. Prior to that, it wasn't too much of a struggle to yield to his perspective, because it often enlarged my own, and more often, we were of one mind.

The details of what happened aren't important; we no longer agreed about anything. It was a tempestuous time. I knew that my teacher was right about my mistakes, but I also felt critical of him. And I was unable to change my direction, even though there were times when I wanted to. I suffered the growing rift between us and the pain it caused for other people. At times, I tried to forget about it and just keep practicing. But that didn't really work either. When I asked other people to help us reconcile, the chasm only deepened.

Finally, my teacher released me from my duties at the Zen center. At a certain point, no other perspectives were available, and no other action could be taken. Anytime we are fired from a position, it is a come-to-Jesus moment. I was confronted with the experience of having failed my teacher and my practice and having been exiled from a community in which I was deeply invested.

For the first time, I saw that I had to let go of my teacher, my community, and most important, my ideas of how our relationship was supposed to be. The Big Mind space helped me traverse this extraordinarily painful separation from the very man who helped me to recognize it so clearly in the first place. Big Mind included every perspective in this conflict but never sided with any of them. There was no conflict—just the powerful coming and going from moment to moment of a relationship that had been very meaningful to me.

Genpo Roshi gave me the dharma name Musho, which translated from the Japanese means "no conflict." Even now, after several years of not seeing each other, he is still teaching me to let go of my ideas of how things should be. We are still connected, because in the space of Big Mind, how could it be otherwise?

All Things Change

According to one of the most important teachings in the Buddhist tradition, all things are subject to context, causes, and conditions, and because of this, they have no intrinsic nature of their own. Everything is always changing. We should learn not to cling to things too tightly (or to people) because they are always in flux, always shifting and changing. Seeing the truth of this is called wisdom.

This is a poetic way of saying that everything in form is dependent on everything else for its existence. For example, my teacher needs students to teach, and we couldn't be students without our teacher. To study Zen, we need Zen masters, sutras, and koans; without genuine seekers, they would have no use at all. To practice, we need to sit, and we depend on our daily rituals and chants to heighten our awareness, harmonize, and deepen our commitment to the Buddha, Dharma, and Sangha. A Zen center doesn't exist if no one is there reciting the Heart Sutra in the morning. Everything is entirely dependent on everything else, like a box and its lid. Genpo Roshi and I needed each other to have our conflict as surely as the foot before needs the foot behind in walking.

At the same time, everything is changing. Nothing is fixed or solid; everything is influencing everything else, and things are always in flux. Our circumstances are changing; therefore, so is our perspective. In one moment, we may feel completely attached to a particular viewpoint, and in the next, we can't remember why it mattered so much. Even so, we all know the tendency to become self-righteous or behave like a know-it-all. We all experience how quickly we can grab onto a particular point of view and make a big deal out of it, snarling like a pit bull that has gotten hold of a pant leg.

Our practice teaches us to let go. It shows us how impermanent and insubstantial our perspectives are. As the scripture says, "Not clinging to them is called transcendent wisdom."

Recognizing that our viewpoints are essentially empty changes how we relate with them. We can still have our opinions and maintain our values, but we cease to grip them as the source of our security and salvation. We learn to hold them relatively, perhaps consistently, but not absolutely. We can make distinctions between commitments and conviction, between ideas and ideology. As we hold our views ever more lightly, we find that we can cultivate and deepen our values because we don't burn out from the fever pitch of asserting our beliefs.

Most important, emptiness is the source of our ability to forgive. Forgiveness happens because things have no intrinsic nature and things change. I can imagine a day sometime in the future when circumstances will have shifted to the point that I will bump into my teacher unexpectedly. We'll give each other a familiar greeting, acknowledge without saying anything that we have both suffered and learned, and proceed from there as though nothing happened, because in a way, it didn't.

PRACTICE

Unbiased Mind

1. Sit for a few minutes identifying with what we call the small self. What do you notice in your mind and body? Where are your boundaries? What is the nature of your thoughts? Your emotions? Where is your attention in time? What are your concerns as the small self? What occupies your attention?

2. Now change your identity and sit for a few minutes as Big Mind. What do you notice now? How big are you? Where are your boundaries? When were you born? When will you die? What do you include in the space of your identity? What do you prefer? What is your feeling state? Can you look at the small self from the space of Big Mind? What do you see?

13

Negotiation

It is never too late to get out of a bad deal.
NOLAND SCHNEIDER, MY FRIEND'S FATHER

THIS WAS THE MANTRA of my good friend's father. He repeated it constantly to her in between trips to Vegas, during business breakfasts in Germany, and after struggling with bows in Tokyo. She took her worldly father's advice to heart. She is one of the best negotiators I know. Every transaction in her life is an opportunity to suggest creative trade-offs, to bargain, and to make deals.

When it was time to renew her insurance policy, she had a vigorous conversation with the insurance company, and they agreed to lower her premium in exchange for a higher deductible. She bought a hat from a Tibetan shop owner, and by the end of their conversation, the man with the compassionate eyes behind the counter threw in a silk medicine bag and a *mala* (Buddhist prayer beads) because he enjoyed his exchange with her so much.

She once negotiated over a vacuum for three years. Her imported vacuum, an expensive blue Miele, didn't work very well, so she took it to the vacuum shop for repair. The shop was run by an older gentleman, an incorrigible and extravagantly dishonest Christian, she said, who advertised free Bibles on his sign out front. He convinced her to trade her older vacuum in on a less expensive, brand-new orange one. On her way out, the assistant, a steady, clear, angelic man, whispered, "Bring it back any time."

After a week or two, she decided that the orange vacuum was, indeed, inferior to the old blue one, so she took the assistant's advice and brought it back. In the meantime, the shop owner had sold her original blue Miele, so the bargaining continued. This time the shop owner agreed to take back the orange vacuum, and for a little more money, she could take home another model, a silver Miele.

As the angelic assistant loaded it into her car, he whispered, "Bring it back any time." The silver vacuum didn't work any better than the old blue one did, and every time she vacuumed, she cursed the Christian man with his free Bibles.

Two years later, she decided to take the silver vacuum back. The corrupt Christian shop owner had died (which made her happy), and now the angelic assistant was running the store. He reprimanded her for gloating about the previous owner's passing, then opened up the negotiations again. She told him the silver vacuum had not done a good job, and because of its canister with the dangling hose, it was cumbersome to pull around. What she really desired was one of those simple, upright Mieles that are easy to move from room to room and from floor to floor.

The angelic assistant said she could have the brand-new vacuum, upright and red, for only an additional $289. But she said no. She had paid the shop enough money already. He then offered it to her for $249. "Nope," she said. Finally, he looked at her and said, "Give me $200 cash, and it's yours." She went straight to the ATM, got the cash, and has been happily vacuuming with her red upright ever since.

Not everyone derives as much pleasure from negotiating as my friend. She is most at home in bazaars and open-air markets and at fairs and art festivals in cities like Seattle and Istanbul, where people throw fish in the air and expect to bargain. She sees the world as filled with creative possibility. She likes the human contact, the pushing and pulling, even the arguments and white lies, but most important, she looks forward to the moment when a new outcome bursts into form. She says, "Negotiating is participating in the creative nature of reality." She doesn't mind disappointment; it comes with the territory. But then, she doesn't always expect to win. In that respect, she is different from her father. She's happier.

Getting to Yes

During my training in mediation, all mediators and negotiators were reading *Getting to Yes: Negotiating Agreement without Giving In,* a best seller by Harvard negotiators Roger Fisher and William R. Ury. The book instructed readers in a win-win approach that focused on how to benefit all parties rather than conventionally assuming that someone must win while the others must lose.[1]

Not that I mind winning and losing, but collaborative negotiation is more like playing jazz than football. The assumption is that something good will emerge if people bring their passion and skills to the table and suspend their need to know how things will turn out, like a good musician who values beauty above all. Collaborative negotiations lower anxiety levels because we don't expend precious life force protecting ourselves from being eaten alive by the other side or, conversely, planning how to eat them.

After reading *Getting to Yes,* I went to Harvard and took Fisher and Ury's weeklong negotiation course. It was excellent training, and they offered some priceless pointers about facilitating win-win negotiations. Whether you were interested in negotiating a land deal, selling a company, settling a lawsuit, or trying to get along with your in-laws during the holidays, Fisher and Ury had a lot to offer, and in fine Harvard style, they delivered.

They taught that all of us are involved in negotiations all the time. Good negotiations depend on cultivating good relationships, so we should be rigorously ethical in our deal making and treat people well. They stressed the importance of preparing for a negotiation by taking different perspectives: yours, the other side's, and a neutral one. They led exercises in which we role-played the position of the other side, looking at the issues from their point of view throughout the negotiation. They helped us to examine what would happen if we walked away from a negotiation and to think about alternatives to reaching an agreement. They also stressed the importance of precise and ample communications, clear and concrete agreements, and well-crafted contracts. We practiced boiling down complex agreements to the simplest terms possible.

Positions

The concept at the heart of *Getting to Yes* is learning how to shift our attention from "positions" to "interests." In most negotiations, we begin by staking out our position, or the outcome we are seeking.

Our eldest daughter, Evan, who is newly married and lives in San Francisco, recently celebrated her thirtieth birthday over Labor Day weekend. Two months before, her husband, Beau, invited us to the big party he was throwing for her.

Earlier that summer, my husband, Michael, had left his law firm to start his own practice. By mid-August, he was remodeling the office, hiring staff and associates, working out new billing procedures, and transferring clients to the new firm. He and his associates were also preparing for some important hearings scheduled for the week after Labor Day. He was madly busy and reluctantly concluded that he probably shouldn't take time off for the party.

As you can imagine, our daughter was extremely disappointed.

She protested that she would only turn thirty once and that her husband had put a great deal of effort into planning the party. If her father had time to fly around the country on frequent business trips, why couldn't he manage a short trip to San Francisco? He had a history of changing his scheduled time with her at the last minute, and she concluded that he didn't value their relationship. Having lost her mother to cancer at a young age, she relied on him to stand in for both parents.

She made some valid points; like her father, she is a lawyer with well-developed skills of persuasion and the ability to advocate for herself. When emotionally provoked, she has the rare gift of maintaining her composure without relinquishing one ounce of her rational mind. If it had been up to me, I would have already bought our plane tickets.

At first, it looked like an impasse. Privately I marveled at the modern luxury of contemplating flying somewhere for a weekend birthday party and the good fortune of my husband, who had the freedom and money to open his own law firm. For the most part, I remained neutral; the territory seemed fraught with emotional land mines, so I stood still and waited for something to change. Both positions were strong and valid, and in the dangerous territory of family dynamics, someone would likely come out hurt or resentful. I didn't want to get caught in the cross fire.

A negotiation always emerges from the eruption of natural forces that act on each other like water on rock. These interactions are constant and create some of the most stunning forms in nature. The action never ceases, and change is perpetual, which is true for us too. Conflict results from this constant flex and flow; initially it often looks insoluble, because that is the nature of opposing positions. Within that opposition, however, exists the opportunity and necessity of negotiation. Time and again with willing parties, I have witnessed the creative transformation of abrasive rock into something smooth, polished, and unique.

Interests

As I said earlier, we have to overcome our aversion to conflict, which derives from our belief that nothing good can come of it. The trick to making this shift, as Fisher and Ury point out, is to look for interests, the underlying wants and needs that drive the original position of each party.

With Evan and Michael, the positions were clear: a daughter's father should travel to an important birthday party; a man should stay home to take care of his business. But what were their respective interests? In other words, what desires were they trying to satisfy with their respective positions?

Evan wanted a meaningful birthday party, full of family as well as friends. It was essential to her to feel loved and supported by her father (and by me), and she wanted her husband's efforts to be rewarded with our presence. She cared deeply about keeping her family intact, particularly in light of losing her mother at such a young age, and this meant honoring familial commitments. Finally, she wanted to feel that her father valued their relationship as much as she did.

Michael, on the other hand, wanted to launch a successful new firm and fulfill his obligations to the business and his partners. Of course, he loves his daughter and wanted her to feel loved and supported and to have a festive birthday. And he sincerely appreciated the value she placed on the well-being of her family; he felt that his professional success was essential to that.

Evan also wanted the launch of her dad's new firm to be successful. When she recognized this shared interest, the whole conversation began to shift. She saw that her father's interests and her own were no longer pitted against each other. Instead, they shared the same dilemma. With this recognition, they moved from sitting opposite each other to sitting on the same side of the table. Then they could focus on the challenge in front of them rather than on the problem between them.

People will often relax their positions when their deeper wants and needs are affirmed. Many times, these wants and needs are subjective; that is to say, they are not concrete or measurable. For example, we want our opinions to be heard and to feel valued and respected. We want to be treated as though we matter. A lot changes in a negotiation when these subjective interests are met.

I can imagine significant protests from readers about how "real" negotiations involving large amounts of money, land, or other resources are anything but cooperative. They are tests of the survival of the fittest and rarely address the subjective interests or higher values of participants. They are, as the saying goes, "all about the money."

True enough. Sometimes negotiations are all about the money, except in those cases when they are not. Either or both can be true. Even in business, it is possible to address the subjective and objective interests of customers, suppliers, employees, shareholders, and other stakeholders, including the well-being of the environment and the larger community, and still be profitable. More and more companies today are discovering that they are more profitable when they do just that—Whole Foods, Southwest Airlines, and Trader Joe's, to name just a few. Like these forward-looking companies, we are capable of enlarging our view of what a good deal actually is.

There is plenty of greed in the world and ruthless competition, no doubt. But there is also an abundance of generosity, goodwill, and a terrific amount of cooperation that serves the whole. Each of us knows what it is like to surrender a hard and fast position in exchange for genuine harmony or to release others from a difficult demand so that we can share a settlement. In giving, we gain.

Options

Once shared interests are identified, creativity sets in. Mining for the layer of shared interests takes time and good faith, but when you hit it, the creative options bubble up like crude oil from the ground.

Suddenly everyone feels like they are enriched; there is plenty to go around. Possibilities keep opening up; ideas flow. This is as true for business negotiations as it is for those involving family.

In Evan and Michael's conversation, the focus shifted from disappointment to the excitement of the shared enterprise of making both events successful—her birthday party and his business opening. They started brainstorming. The only criterion was to meet their shared interests. Maybe he could fly to the party and return the same day. Maybe they could Skype during the party. Maybe she could fly to Salt Lake City later and celebrate a belated birthday, and he could pay for it!

The ideas flowed back and forth, and they agreed he would Skype her during the birthday party, and he would also travel to San Francisco later that fall and take her out to celebrate. Not only did it turn out well, but that birthday Skype call between Evan and her dad became a family ritual. We now have a weekly, early Sunday morning video conference with the whole family. Everyone likes it. You can tell because all four of our kids are willing to get up early, stagger to their laptop computers in jersey pajama bottoms, sweatshirts, and bed heads, with big mugs of coffee, yawning and teasing. It is very sweet. The combination of Evan's water and Michael's stone has brought our family a new and beautiful form of intimacy.

PRACTICE

Looking for Interests

1. The next time you find yourself in a negotiation, take a moment to acknowledge the position that you have taken and also the position of the other side. It could be a simple negotiation involving family, friends, or your landlord, or it could be a complex one involving a contract or business transaction.
2. Take a piece of paper and draw a line down the center. Write your name at the upper left-hand side of the paper and the other person's name at the upper right.

3. Write your position below your name in the left-hand column. Write the position of the other side in the right-hand column. Do they look incompatible?

4. Now ask yourself, "What wants or needs will be satisfied by my position? What wants or needs will be satisfied by the other side's position?" List them.

5. Circle all of the interests that appear on both sides of the line.

6. Generate a list of options that will satisfy these shared interests.

14

Conflict and Creativity

Every single moment of existence is a creative act.
KEN WILBER[1]

EVERY CULTURE HAS its creation story. In ours, the universe exploded
13.7 billion years ago from absolute nothingness into stunning existence, a grand display of the ceaseless, dynamic activity of form emerg-
ing, evolving, and dissolving again. In the vast, silent space between
stars, there are constant fireworks, a flurry of violent eruptions and volatile changes bursting with urgency and frothing with evolving forms.

The universe is not a gentle place. Rather, it is a creative ex-
travaganza filled with light and energy. Creativity is all-pervasive and
ever present, tumultuous, and exciting. Creativity is, in part, another
name for evolution, because evolution is the very mechanism of new
forms coming into being. Ken Wilber describes the evolution of the
universe and its creative imperative this way:[2]

Fourteen billion years ago there was, as far as physicists can tell,
more or less absolutely nothing, just simply nothing. And then,

Boom! We had the Big Bang and the fundamental aspects of the material universe, as we know them, blew into existence. And this is an extraordinary event, because all of a sudden, something exists. Where before there was nothing, now we have this world of material particles.

Not only that, we now have all of the particles given that will ever be given and which form the basic building blocks of everything to come; the pouring out of more and more creative acts. And it begins with something like strings. Then strings come together as quarks, and then quarks gather together and form electrons and protons and neutrons, and these bind to create atoms, and atoms coalesce to form molecules.

Then in one of the most amazing and impossible-to-fathom miracles ever, these strings of several dozen different types of molecules come together. A cell membrane drops around these molecules and all of a sudden, the creative emergence of cells occurs, and the beginning of all life appears. In other words, life springs forward from insentient matter.

Life moves from simple sensation and perception in a single cell to a reptilian brain stem, a paleomammalian limbic system, a cortex, and a neocortex, and very soon human beings appear in their earliest forms, about a million years ago. The modern version of our species came on line about 175,000 years ago. Each advance in the nervous systems of life forms in turn creates greater capacity for consciousness, and in that way the Kosmos becomes more and more sensitive to itself. In other words, the universe becomes self-aware through the perception of its own creations.

We humans are still in the process of evolving. It's not just that our exteriors have changed: we walk on two feet instead of four; we have a larger brain and a smaller brow and teeth; and for better or worse, females are fertile year-round. One look at our advertising and that much is obvious.

Our interiors—our capacity for language and cognition; our beliefs and worldviews; our values, needs, and motivations—are also evolving. Human beings have begun to contemplate evolution, to observe evolution, even as we are part of it. This is a tremendous innovation in consciousness. As we begin to see the extraordinary journey of our species, we integrate into our awareness, which prepares us to consciously participate in the next creative step of our unfolding.

Most people assume that creativity is limited to humans and then usually to a select few; namely, the artistic, philosophical, and scientific geniuses. But Ken Wilber reminds us that in our universe, creativity is anything but rare. It occurs in the moment-to-moment existence of everyone and everything. Since we are born of the natural creativity of life, we always possess it. Just like the universe, we are endowed with the God-like ability to manifest form from emptiness and fashion the material of our world into ever new and different combinations. Creativity is in the hard drive of our existence. We can't help but create, so it is essential to continuously pose to ourselves the question, "What is it that we are creating?"

Creative Opportunity

In conflict situations, we rarely ask ourselves that question. Instead, we focus on what is being inflicted upon us or what we are being forced to endure. But if we are part of this universe, then every situation we are in, including moments of conflict and struggle, brings something fresh and offers us an opportunity to innovate.

So how do we learn to see our conflicts as creative opportunities? How do we reinterpret the hardwired bodily sensations signaling threat and the need for protection as the unruly excitement of the creative process at work? How do we shift the perception of ourselves as a prisoner of our conflicts to a partner in creative resolution? And how might we invoke the curiosity and exploration usually associated with artists, giving ourselves the freedom to imagine and create new ways of working with our challenges?

There are many extraordinary examples of innovation in conflict resolution—from large social movements to small, intimate gestures between friends. Every attempt to react differently establishes new pathways for others to step into when faced with conflict.

When apartheid was abolished in South Africa, the new government faced a daunting task: how to address the impacts of suffering due to long-standing policies of racism and oppression. Some daring people, such as Archbishop Desmond Tutu, decided that simply speaking truth was the one action that could move the nation forward from the injury of the past.

They designed a process, overseen by the Truth and Reconciliation Commission, in which perpetrators of violence could forgo punishment in exchange for telling the truth about what had happened. Although many thought this to be impossible, the Truth and Reconciliation Commission actually succeeded in setting a new course for the future for the country. South Africa still faces many challenges in establishing a just society, but the commission has become a model for others throughout the world. It is an example of a new groove in human culture for dealing with a history of injustice and trauma.

In my years as a mediator, I saw many creative responses to working with conflicts. One example was the victim-offender mediation program that we implemented in our court system. Based on earlier models around the country, this program involved juveniles who had already pleaded guilty to a crime but were willing to negotiate issues of restitution. With the help of a trained facilitator, the offending youths would sit down and talk forthrightly with those who had been injured by their actions. They would explore motivations and mistakes and imagine all kinds of ways to make things right.

These were amazing conversations, and I frequently witnessed the emergence of creative solutions that no court would be allowed to impose. Young people would make spontaneous apologies; offer to clean up, repair, or pay for damage they had done to property; and express genuine empathy with the people they had hurt. After one such negotiation, a business owner hired a youth to work for the very company he had vandalized because he was so impressed with the teenager's efforts to make amends. Juveniles who participated in these mediation sessions were three times more likely to fulfill their agreements than to comply with orders from the court.

Creativity is always percolating just below the surface of our lives. It just needs a chance to bubble up. We can create the conditions for greater creativity by first bringing our attention directly to the problem with the express purpose of exploring its dimensions with an open and positive mind.

Imagine for a moment a situation in which you are having trouble with a colleague at work. Perhaps you have noticed that your conversations have become strained, or you sense tension between the two of you. Our habitual response would be to avoid the problem, talk about it with mixed success, or hope it goes away.

But by bringing the situation forward in our minds and becoming present to it, we are already allowing the possibility for creativity to emerge—that is, as long as the mind stays willing. We will, of course, experience discomfort and may be tempted to withdraw. But this is an opportunity to reinterpret the sensations of tension and to familiarize ourselves with the anxiety that frequently attends the creative process. Every artist must know how to embrace tension; it is part and parcel of creativity. Give it a try. Just for a few minutes.

The next step is to play with the conflict in your imagination as a child plays with a toy. I use the word *play* intentionally, because it implies an attitude of ease, curiosity, and possibility. In the realm of playful imagination, anything is possible. As my grandfather used to say, "All you need is your own consent."

Imagine several scenarios. See yourself and your colleague sitting together at a table at work, standing next to each other and looking out of a large window, or riding along together on a donkey in cowboy hats. It's up to you. Make it up. It's fun. Maybe you need to clear some aggression from the scene. So if you must, inhabit a cartoon aggression (to diffuse the aggression rather than fuel it) and pull out a play club from under your coat and bop your colleague on the head. Then allow them to bop you.

Now that you have the fight out of the way, it is crucial to imagine yourself in a positive context, laughing together or working intently and successfully on a shared problem. Think about having a really satisfying conversation, beginning with appreciation of each other's work, and then exchanging genuine feedback in an atmosphere of respect. Add a background of a night sky and stars to your conversation—anything to enhance the atmosphere with possibility and beauty. What do you imagine saying to that person? What would you like them to say to you? Can you feel how engaging lightly with the problem in your mind is already affecting your experience of the situation?

Now, and this is important, just forget about it for a time. In every model of creativity that I am familiar with, there is a stage in which the problem is simply put away and left to the unconscious to work on. In some models, it is called incubation; in others, the space in between brainstorming sessions. From a mediator's point of view, this is simply relinquishing our attachment to controlling outcomes and trusting instead the great space of unconditioned awareness that is the source of all things. With patience and trust, an insight, a new idea, or a creative response will often be thrown up onto the shores of your imagination.

I was offered a very sweet gift from that source after a falling out with a longtime male friend. We were gym buddies and movie friends, and we talked regularly on the phone. I must have done or said something to offend him (I still don't know what), but suddenly he wasn't talking to me anymore. He seemed to drop right out of my life. I didn't know what had happened, so I left him several voice messages, asking him to call me back. Nothing. I felt hurt and bewildered by his absence.

After a few months had passed, I began to let go of the friendship and was making peace with my loss. One rainy afternoon, I went with Willie to a ceramic shop to make pottery. It was a dreamy, gray day, and I enjoyed sitting next to him while he worked, his chubby hands covered in clay, peering down at his project through thick glasses. I was sitting next to him, glazing a simple white vase while raindrops pelted the window. As I painted away, I suddenly found myself writing the word *Mercy* across the surface of the base in strong, black letters. It wasn't something I did intentionally; rather, the word just seemed to pass through my imagination onto the surface of the pot, almost before I noticed. *Hm,* I thought. *Mercy.*

Later, as I picked up the vase after it had been fired in the kiln, it occurred to me that I had painted it for my friend. How interesting. It was a simple and beautiful vase, deep red with shiny, bold letters. I decided to give it to him. I bought a bouquet of flowers, put them in the pot, and left it on his front porch. A few hours later, I received a call from him, happy and renewed. Problem solved.

You may not have confidence in the power of your imagination; if you don't, just consider your dreams. They occur every night, whether you remember them or not, and they are proof positive of the extraordinary gifts of imagination. James Watson and Francis Crick discovered the structure of DNA after Watson dreamed of an image of spiral staircases. Writers and artists have always looked to their dreams as sources of inspiration: Salvador Dali and Frida Kahlo transferred their dream images directly to the canvas. Mary Shelley dreamed the idea of Frankenstein before she wrote the novel. Robert Louis Stevenson "saw" Dr. Jekyll and Mr. Hyde in a dream. Stephen King has said his dreams inform his fiction.

Dreams also carry messages, reveal meanings, and frequently offer us direction for our dilemmas. Once I had a dream that helped resolve a burdensome conflict. I had enrolled Willie in an alternative public school in which the parents played a large role in the classroom. Although there were no children with disabilities in the program, initially they were happy to accept Willie and his best friend, Isaac, who also has Down syndrome. Midway through their first semester, the principal unexpectedly called me, informing me they had changed their minds, and Willie would not be allowed to continue in the program after the New Year.

As every parent of a child with a disability knows, it is an ongoing struggle to create a place for your child in school and the culture at large. In spite of all our good intentions, including the Americans with Disabilities Act, we still marginalize people with disabilities, relegating them to the back room.

From one point of view, I understood the position of the principal. I am sure she and her staff either were encountering extra work they hadn't anticipated or were perhaps fearful of a flood of special-needs children applying to the program. Still, the law had created protections and opportunities for my son that I shouldn't have to fight for.

I remember vividly the impact on my body when I received the phone call. The energy completely drained out of me. I felt lost and deflated and simply didn't know what to do. Should I accept my child being thrown out of his elementary school, or should I find a way to stand up for him, throwing all of my weight against the decision made by the principal and her staff? To be honest, I couldn't even think about it. I couldn't talk about it. I felt heartsick, weak, and empty. All I wanted to do was cry. I didn't have the energy to even imagine doing something about it.

That night I dreamed I was walking in a beautiful garden when suddenly I came upon a saddle buried in the earth. It was a very strange image, yet its meaning was immediately clear to me. I knew that the dream was telling me to "mount up" and go forward on behalf of my son. The beauty of the garden assured me that the situation was fertile. I woke up positively renewed to face the challenge. Indeed, after several intense meetings with the principal and some of her teachers, I succeeded in persuading them to keep my son in the program, and for the next six years, he and his friend were very happy there, and the faculty and other students were happy to have them.

When we face our conflicts, invite our imagination to interact with them, and then give them up to the great space of Creativity itself, new ideas and insights burst forward unexpectedly. It is our work to capture those ideas, to try them out, and to struggle to bring them into form.

Creativity Takes Work

The idea is not to eliminate conflict; I cannot stress this enough. The aim is to transform it. Evolution is a messy business. While inspiration comes suddenly, dramatically, even mystically, more often, new ways of being require commitment and time and patience, all of which must be harnessed to a steady vision. The creative process necessarily involves encounters with the unknown, the chaotic, and the pain that seems to accompany the birth of something new. To experience the joy and excitement of that birth, we must be willing to experience unpleasant emotions—from empty irritation to boredom, frustration, and even despair.

We must cultivate creativity. Each moment in time is infused with the fresh, the new, the possible, but it is also heavily laden with past conditioning: our evolutionary history as primates, the mores of our culture, our family upbringing, and wounds from previous relationships. So we may have to push through deeply ingrained habits of body and mind to begin to touch the possible.

Finally, we have to be prepared to fail. Again and again. It is intrinsic to the creative process. Every successful person is a student of failure. It has often been said that failure is only the opportunity to begin again.

An artist friend once told me that the greatest difficulty in painting is getting rid of the part that is holding back the rest. When he became attached to a particular part of a painting, he couldn't complete the work. Once when he was stuck like this, he asked a friend to help. He left the studio and when he came back, she had painted out ninety percent of what he had created. He sat down and cried. And then he began painting again.

PRACTICE

Conflict and Creativity

1. Bring a conflict into your awareness with the intention of working creatively with it.
2. View any discomfort in your body or mind as the tug and pull of the creative process, and allow it just to be there.
3. Play with the situation in your imagination. Move the players in your scenario around. Give them outfits, environments, different scripts to recite. You can create anything you want in this scene. Just start to imagine, but be sure that your scenario is giving you a positive feeling state.
4. Now relinquish your project to open space. Just drop it into the creative reservoir of the unknown and wait until something emerges for you. Pay attention to your dreams, where answers may pop up.
5. Capture any insights or new approaches that begin to emerge.
6. Try your idea out. Expect that it might fail. Refine it. Try it again.

15

Reframing: The Power
of Interpretation

The greatest discovery of my generation is that a human being
can alter his life by altering his attitudes of mind.
WILLIAM JAMES[1]

THE PRESIDENT AND THE POPE were out boating on a lake. The
pope was wearing his miter, that tall liturgical hat that reaches up
toward heaven, giving him that powerful, papal presence. A big wind
came up and swept the miter off his head into the water. Oops. The
president, quick and cool, climbed out of the boat, walked across the
water, picked up the miter, and shaking the water off of it, brought
it back to the pope. The next day the headlines read, "The president
can't swim."

In the media, reframing is called "spin." We all know what it's
like to listen to the same news event interpreted by different news
channels. We can hardly believe that the talking heads are referring

to the same thing. But it shows us just how powerful and flexible the mind is; the same event can be interpreted in many ways.

The "frame," or interpretation, we put on our experience determines its meaning to us, but we often don't recognize that we are, in fact, interpreting. We assume that our interpretations are the way it is. Marcel Duchamp, one of the most influential artists of the twentieth century, shocked us into seeing the power of the frame by taking a urinal and placing it in a museum. Suddenly, this mundane, functional object took on an entirely new meaning. By doing this, Duchamp shifted our perspective and, even more, challenged our definitions of art.

We reframe whenever we consciously reshape the meaning of events, relationships, and circumstances in our lives. It is very powerful and, like magic, can be used for good or ill. In the context of conflict resolution, when leveraged with positive intent, it is golden.

As a mediator, I frequently used reframes to validate the truths of someone's experience, while simultaneously opening up different ways to understand and work with those same truths. One skillful reframe can determine whether a conversation succeeds or fails. I recall a session from some years ago in which a reframe did just that.

The mediation involved the administrative assistant for a construction company and her coworker, who was a project manager. She worked in the office, while he was usually out on the job site. But they crossed paths in the morning and at day's end, and they needed to communicate about hours on the job, paying workers, billing, and so on.

For some unknown reason, they had grown increasingly critical and irritable with each other to the point that they avoided talking altogether. The situation had become intolerable for their boss, the owner of the company, who respected and valued them both but who had been unable to budge them on the issue that was festering between them.

He called me to arrange a mediation session and required them both to show up. Neither wanted to be there, and the atmosphere was tense. After my opening remarks, I asked who wanted to begin. They agreed she would start. So I turned to her to open the discussion, asking her to describe the problem from her perspective.

She looked across the table at her coworker, then looked back at me and said flatly, "I think he's an arrogant jerk."

Wow, I thought. *That was not helpful.* Her attack took me by surprise, as I am sure it did him, and I wondered for a moment what to do about it. I took a moment to tease out her meaning in my mind, and I offered her this reframe.

"Well," I said, "whatever he is, it sounds like you don't feel respected."

"That's right," she said. "I don't feel respected," and she stopped there. I could feel her soften as she sank down in her chair and lowered her gaze. He visibly relaxed as she turned from confronting him to expressing her feelings to me.

Two things happened in that reframe that changed the atmosphere in the room and turned the conversation toward a positive outcome. First, we shifted the subject of the conversation away from the negative complaint of arrogance to the positive value of respect, which relieved her. This was because, as I found out later, she actually liked and respected this man a great deal and was hurt by the distance between them.

Second, when we moved the focus from the attack on him toward exploring her experience instead, this gave him the room to empathize with her and to explore the situation from his side without being defensive. He explained that, while he wasn't sure what had created the chasm, the more he felt her unhappiness with him, the more he stayed away. What she regarded as arrogance or lack of respect was simply steering clear of trouble.

We never did find the source of the original rift, but it didn't seem to matter. They simply needed to clear the air and start fresh. They validated each of their points of view, reestablished their connection, and restored their mutual respect. Then we made some simple agreements about communicating in the future. I think we talked for about an hour and a half that day, and they left my office like two people who had worked well together for years. Not all mediations end so smoothly, but these people had a long history of cooperation before the problem set in.

We can use reframing for many different purposes. We can use it to shift from looking at issues from a short-term perspective to a longer one. "My husband and I don't communicate well" becomes "My husband and I don't communicate well, yet" or "at the moment." Now the statement is about a living relationship, and it affirms the possibility of improvement.

We can use reframing to reduce threatening language or attacks. An accusation like "You are too aloof or too emotionally distant" can evoke a more neutral response like "I know I'm self-contained," or "I tend to be introverted, and I'm sorry if that is challenging."

Skillful reframes can help us strip the negative judgments from our conversations, drain off the threatening energy, and introduce more mercy and trust into the effort to work out our differences. For example, "You're too intense" becomes "I'm really passionate; it's true." The criticism "You're too easily swayed by others," can be received with "I do like lots of input," and toned down by adding, "There may be times when it is too much." "You are so stubborn" can be acknowledged and reframed as "I admit that I take strong positions." All of these reinterpretations create the space for a downshift in negativity and a productive conversation that results in some agreement.

Reframing is more than just an exercise in semantics, however. It is more than making a positive statement out of a negative one. The reframes that sugarcoat experience don't stick. A common complaint like "You're never home, and all I do is run around taking care of everything" cannot be turned into "I'm a domestic adventurer." Sorry, people, this won't work. To succeed, a reframe has to contain a compelling truth.

However, that first statement can be reframed as "I really value our time together and want more of it." Or "I prefer it when we work together." Or "I want to feel that we are sharing the workload fairly." Most people wouldn't argue with these statements. First, because they are first-person "I" statements, free of blame and finger-pointing, and second, because they assert a positive intention. The reframe can now become the basis for a rich exploration of our respective roles in the family: our satisfactions, our discontents, and our agreements about sharing labor. That is, if we are willing. New interpretations won't work when they are sentimental or glib; rather, they must enrich or deepen our perspective, enabling us to see more than we did before, not less.

One of my students is working on becoming more awake to his emotional states, giving himself permission to feel more deeply and to express his feelings. It is something his girlfriend wants from him, and he agrees. But he says that when she asks him how he is feeling in the moment, he struggles to answer her question.

"Honestly," he says, "I'm like a deer in the headlights. I really don't know how I feel a lot of the time. I freeze, unable to access my body signals immediately, let alone describe those feelings on the spot." His girlfriend accuses him of being "too heady," and the label leaves him feeling deflated and defensive.

For him, learning to access and talk about his feelings is like learning a second language. Rationality is his mother tongue. There's nothing wrong with his style of communication; in fact, it is his strong suit. So we reframed "overly heady" to "powerfully rational," which he is, and he felt supported by this. He is still inspired to learn to include his feeling sense in his communications, and he is more because of it, not less.

Feelings Remixed

It is much more difficult to reframe experience when it is accompanied by strong feelings. If we are angry, hurt, embarrassed, or filled with anxiety, these states often govern the meaning we make of our experiences. Not that there is anything wrong with getting mad or having a down day. But it is far more challenging to reframe meaning when our nervous system is flooded with uncomfortable sensations. So we can learn to reframe the feelings themselves.

One of my female students is practicing reframing her feelings of jealousy. When she begins to date someone, she becomes possessive after a couple of weeks, a few phone calls, and a drink or two. She finds herself suddenly expecting exclusivity from her new companion when, rationally, that's not what she wants. She is highly aware that jealousy and insecurity are a turnoff to everybody, including herself. So she has been doing therapy to look more deeply into this pattern.

She told me recently that she had a breakthrough when she discovered that she could reframe her feeling states. Now when the jealousy comes up, instead of running to see if the new man in her life is posting pictures of someone else on Facebook, she reinterprets her impulse.

First, she is practicing getting to know her own feelings intimately. She no longer takes the jealousy literally, but instead becomes curious about the precise signals in her body. What are they? Where are they? How exactly do they feel?

She takes the time to bring her attention to the nausea in her stomach and the achy sensation in her chest that she calls pining. She can now distinguish the grip of anger along her jaw that runs down the back of her neck as a need for control. She watches the feelings shift and change. As she becomes familiar with them and their instability, she is learning to breathe and relax, which allows her to stay present with their ebb and flow. You might say she is learning to surf her own jealousy.

Finally, she has changed her whole attitude toward that jealousy, befriending it rather than criticizing herself for it. She has reframed the feelings as signals of her desire to preserve a loving relationship, one that is safe and honest. While she still needs to curb the behaviors of jealousy, these uncomfortable feelings now cue her to focus on her desire for loyalty rather than on her fear of betrayal.

She says it is much easier to work with the jealous feelings when she sees their positive function rather than interpreting them as a negative affliction to be overcome. She no longer feels bad about herself, but she is excited about the adventure of looking inward. I've told her that if she can learn to stay present to jealousy with its complex mix of passion and aggression, she can stay present to any emotion.

What Is Right?

If we want to learn to reframe, it is simple to do. To begin, we simply identify a troubling or irritating trait in ourselves—or even easier, in someone else. We just pay attention to the situation and our reactions to it, like my student is doing with her jealousy. Learning to be fully present to exactly the way things appear to us, as well as our responses to them, is the heart of all awareness practice: "My boss is dominating, and I resent it." "My girlfriend is always late, and I'm irritated by it." "My team is disorganized, and I lose inspiration." "The country is moving in the wrong direction, and I'm scared."

To catalyze a reframe, ask what is *right* about the situation. What is the intelligence in the way things are now?

That is the question I asked myself when the construction company administrator called her coworker an arrogant jerk. What was right about her experience? She was upset, that was for sure. She was accusing him of being arrogant. Indeed. Arrogance means putting yourself above others. So I wondered if she was feeling put down. But what was right about it? Well, she wanted to feel like they are equals; she wanted to be respected. So I said to her, "It sounds like you don't feel respected." It was a reframe that empathized with her struggle, honored her positive intention, but freed everyone from the dead end of her criticism. And because it rang true, the reframe succeeded.

Sometimes discovering what is right about our situation is our only good option. I remember an old story from the Sufi tradition in which a person who is struggling with weeds in his garden goes to the master gardener for help. The first time, the master gardener suggests some amendments to the soil, along with changing the watering cycle. But it doesn't work, and the weeds come back. So the person goes back a second time for more advice. The master gardener suggests introducing a different plant into the garden, one known to ward off weeds. This strategy also fails. The frustrated gardener returns to the master a third time, and the master asks, "You changed the soil?"

"Yes."

"You adjusted the water?"

"Yes."

"You added the new plants?"

"Yes."

"And the weeds are still there?"

"Yes."

"Well, then I suggest that you learn to love them."

It is one thing to reframe a complaint or criticism, it is another to reframe your life.

PRACTICE

Reframing

1. Identify a persistent, irksome complaint in your life.
2. Feel its qualities directly.
3. Now ask, "What is right about this?" See if you can identify the positive side of the situation.
4. If you are working on a reframe regarding someone else, shift the subject to "I."

16

Giving and Receiving Feedback

Be yourself; the world will give you feedback.
CHÖGYAM TRUNGPA[1]

LET'S BE CLEAR. I don't want "feedback." But I understand how necessary it is for effective collaboration and intimacy and for keeping relationships alive and well. Still, whenever someone gets that I-want-to-give-you-feedback look in their eye, equanimity flees. I suddenly feel like I am sixteen, and my sense of self is as fragile as a little bird. Instantly, up come the defenses—the flight, fight, or freeze responses. The little bird in me flies off, the burly badger bears its teeth, or the small rabbit freezes in the brush.

The good news is that, for the most part, the instincts of my ego's natural defenses no longer run the show. Since I know my life is not literally threatened, I have learned to relax, using my breath to calm my activated, overly protective nervous system. Sometimes I have the wherewithal to remind myself quietly to give the other person the prerogative of their own perspective and to become curious about what they have to say to me.

The practice of receiving feedback is, in some ways, similar to the practice of sitting on the meditation cushion. Breath after breath, we relax our deeply held attachment to our sense of self and to the never-ending commentary about "me." We open our heart to the moment and enter into the wilderness of a greater identity—unknown, expansive, and liberated.

In our relationships, we can experience the same openness and freedom. As our grip on our identity loosens, we become more fearless in communicating with others, trusting in our ability to work with what is coming our way. We learn to stay put and relax rather than darting away, confronting, or ignoring the threat that a relationship poses.

Receiving Feedback: Three Options

Receiving feedback is an art, just as giving it is; in both cases, we need to hone our sense of timing. When someone offers us a reflection about who we are, invited or not, we need to slow down our habitual sense of time and allow a short interval for our body to experience the threat.

I like to use the analogy of playing tennis. If somebody hits the ball over the net, you have to back up and prepare to receive the ball. Unless, of course, you charge the net. But in interpersonal communication, a volley is usually unhelpful, so you watch the ball bounce. You back up, retract your forehand, and prepare to make the return. This interval gives you the space to respond consciously.

Usually, we don't allow for the space, so we fail to feel the body's reaction. And when we stop feeling, its sensations start dictating our responses, most often without our knowing it. Learning to feel directly and consciously is a very important part of our awareness practice, particularly when we're trying to learn new skills for dealing with conflict.

Because we often fail to take notice of our bodily responses consciously, we quickly discount what's been said. Recently, I had to tell Willie the sad news that our puppy had been hit by a car. His first response was, "Never mind, Diane. That was a wild dog." He completely discounted any feeling about the loss. This was a strange response for Willie. Usually, he is good at including feeling, but this time, he didn't. He attacked the dog instead. He did something we all have done. He made the dog bad so he wouldn't have to feel the loss.

So we can practice receiving feedback and working with our responses to it. There are three ways to do this.

1. JUST LISTENING TO FEEDBACK

Recently, a student of mine was told by a friend that she is aloof and sometimes difficult to connect to. The student immediately became defensive and hurt, like anyone would in the same situation. But then she put those feelings aside and decided to listen to her friend's point of view without taking issue with it. She listened to what her friend had to say about her own first-person experience; my student did not confuse listening with agreement. So the first way to receive feedback is to listen even when we don't agree.

Active listening includes reflection; you repeat in a natural way what you heard the person say. For instance, if someone says, "You're too aloof," you can respond with, "I hear that you find me aloof." The ego must relax in order for this to be genuine. But the more we practice, the easier it is to do.

Listening to feedback is powerful, because we are giving the speaker the dignity of their experience. It is a very respectful offer, especially when we don't agree. Since it is difficult to listen when we're feeling criticized, our willingness to do so builds trust and contributes to the durability of the relationship. As Rumi says, "Love itself describes its own perfection. Be speechless and listen."[2]

2. REFRAMING FEEDBACK

A second option when receiving feedback is to reframe the feedback in order to soften the judgment. "You are aloof" can become "True, I'm reserved," or "It sounds like we're not as close as you would like." With a more compassionate interpretation, we can find kindness in the exchange. While we may accept a partial truth in the feedback, we don't have to join in with a negative conclusion.

During a divorce mediation, I received a call from the woman, who was having a problem with my facilitation style. She said that she felt upset after our last session because I had been flirting with her husband. *What?* I thought. *Flirting with your husband? Well, I never.* Talk about a flutter in the nervous system. I immediately felt defensive; an imaginary scarlet letter of shame appeared on my chest. I didn't even like her soon-to-be-ex that much, because I found him to be stubborn and difficult to engage in the negotiations.

I took a moment to listen to her critique and felt my urge to defend my virtue. Then a few sarcastic thoughts passed through my mind like, *You're the one who married him, not me.* Soon I relaxed with her feedback and asked myself what partial truth was being expressed. I appreciated her willingness to tell me. After thinking it over for a moment, I said, "I can see how you can think that. From my side, I believe my interactions with him are an attempt to be playful. I feel a need to lighten up the atmosphere. I'm sorry that it's bothering you."

She was immediately pacified by my response. The reframe shifted her experience of our initial interaction, and that is all she seemed to need to move on. She said something simple like, "Oh, fine," and never brought it up again. By the end of our call, I was truly happy that she had brought her concern forward because I learned a lot from it.

I often wonder why I am so quick to defend myself and whether my self-image is really in need of protection. What is this self-concept that I hold, and why is it so furtive? Like most of us, I have built up a lot of defenses around my self-concept, and I am quick to push away any reflection that doesn't conform to my idea of who "I" am.

But at a certain point, even I can acknowledge the relief of surrendering my protection, for then I can sink into the recognition of my own humanness. Opening to feedback can also cut through our spiritual pride, connecting us to our vulnerability and humility and the tenderness of being human. As much as I would like it to be otherwise, I am far from perfect. I share the universal belief that we are supposed to be perfect, and yet not one of us is. As Kobayashi Issa says, "Where there are humans, there are flies, and Buddhas."[3] How perfect is that?

3. OWNING FEEDBACK

I was traveling with a good friend in Nepal. We had just come down from the mountains and arrived in Kathmandu at about 5:00 P.M. It was hot and congested, and we were both irritable. We started to make our way to the hotel. I wanted to look at the map to be sure of the direction, but we only had one and it was in her backpack.

I asked her to pull it out so I could look at it.

"I know where the hotel is," she said, as she kept walking.

I asked her again, and she refused again. Finally, I yelled at her, "Mary, why do you have to be so freaking stubborn?"

"I don't know," she yelled back.

The third approach to receiving feedback, and perhaps the most challenging, is to just take it in, like Mary did. She caught me completely off guard because she agreed with me and made no attempt to argue or defend herself. So I gave in and followed her until she found the hotel—without using the map.

Granted, we can only do this successfully when the feedback rings true. There is an old saying where I am from, "If one person says you are a horse's ass, forget about it. If two people say you are a horse's ass, think about it. If three people say you are a horse's ass, get yourself a saddle." Sometimes people project their own struggles onto us; other times what people tell us is so obvious that, like Mary, we couldn't possibly disagree.

If someone complains of our aloofness, we might respond, "I know. I'm so distant I don't even know where I am." Humor can lighten the interaction, but using it takes practice so it doesn't become a defense. What matters is that we can just laugh at ourselves a bit. Our response doesn't have to be entirely true, just slightly true. As Willie likes to say, "I'm just gonna take the blame here."

If we're accused of being a flirt, we might say, "Yes, I am. I love men, women, people. I flirt with everybody. I can't help myself. It's a sexy, sexy world out there." I'm not sure how this would go over, but I smile thinking about it.

Owning the feedback is something we can play with. In some circumstances, we may want to be apologetic, particularly if we are in touch with how our way of being may create pain in others. Each of us is caught in the predicament that no matter how hard we may try, we are going to cause suffering. Real intimacy is always trimmed with pain.

After Willie was born, my marriage fell apart, which often happens to parents of children with disabilities. Ninety percent of couples divorce after the death of a child or the birth of a child like mine. When we're drowning in grief, it's hard to be present for one another, let alone acknowledge our different styles of dealing with loss.

I felt terrible about separating from my husband. My son was only two, and I knew the impact on him would be irrevocable. I was in great turmoil until a friend of mine said, "Well, it's not like Willie hasn't caused you pain."

This comment stopped me in my tracks, opening me to the recognition that suffering in relationships is unavoidable. It is built into the hard drive of our existence. Mother and baby suffer in the birth process. Siblings can't help but crowd each other out. Friends move on. Loved ones get sick and die.

From this perspective, feedback acknowledges the truth that our differences can hurt. There is nothing to be done about it except be grateful that we can tell the truth.

Giving Feedback

The only thing I like less than receiving feedback is giving it. It is not fun for me. Yet it is integral to my role as a teacher and a manager of an organization, so I practice doing it in ways that can be aptly received by my employees and students while leaving me intact.

Many people in positions of power or leadership may be comfortable giving instructions for a second or third time, offering mixed reviews on performance, or expressing disappointment. Athletic coaches, editors, teachers, supervisors, and parents have to give feedback all day long.

Still, I find it nerve-racking. On one level, my reluctance strikes me as immature. On another level, tension is bound to arise when egoistic boundaries bump into one another and I have to assert my viewpoint. People who know me would be surprised by this admission, because I don't shrink when it comes to saying what I think. Yet internally I have to overcome a lot of resistance to offering even mildly challenging feedback.

Along the way I have learned some things that might be helpful.

Calm. Some of us experience low-level anxiety when giving feedback. So we need to prepare by noticing even small levels of uneasiness. If we are emotionally stressed, calming ourselves is essential. Because we humans are such subtle creatures, our energy communicates much more immediately than our words do, and any anxiety will most likely be interpreted as reproach.

We can soothe the nervous system by reflecting on what we appreciate about the person. Perhaps in recent weeks they have made a good effort. Or perhaps others in the office appreciate what they do. If it's our child, we can recall how much we love them. Such reflections have an immediate, positive effect; they polish our intention and create an atmosphere of goodwill and trust, even in the midst of challenging communications.

Whether you want to begin your feedback with appreciation is up to you. It is always an intuitive call. Sometimes it can grease the skids, making it easier to start a difficult conversation. Other times it can create an awkward moment of waiting for the other shoe to drop. At some point during the interaction, include your praise and appreciation.

Clear and Simple. Once we acknowledge our appreciation, even if it's just internally, we need to express ourselves openly, simply, and clearly. It helps to begin with a good lead-in sentence, such as, "Let's check in about the project," or "Can we take some time to talk about how things are going?" How we shape the opening will depend somewhat on our role. If we are in a position of authority, we don't need the other's consent in order to have the conversation. If we are equals, however, we will have to elicit it.

We should speak with kind confidence. We have to be careful to avoid hedging, stumbling, or apologizing for what we are saying. Sometimes we are too dominating; other times we have a tendency to soften or qualify our statements to take the pressure off, which can make the message ambiguous or ineffective. As the Buddha said, we should tune ourselves like a guitar string: "Not too tight, not too loose."

People deserve our candor and our clarity. It is very important to support what we are saying with a clear description of our expectations, as well as examples of what improvement would look like. Making use of the power of "I" statements, we could say, for example, "I would like the piece posted on the Web in a timely manner. Can we agree that every Monday morning it will go up on the site?" Or, "Our newsletters are sporadic, and their quality is uneven. I would like to create a monthly deadline for their distribution. I have ideas about improving the content, but I would like to hear your ideas first. What do you think would help?"

Mutuality. Finally, I never give feedback without asking questions and checking to see how I have been understood. I want to know what someone has heard me say and how they interpret it. I am curious whether we see things similarly. So I might ask a question like, "What did you hear that is important to you?" or, "What do you agree with, and what do you disagree with?"

Finding shared understanding in our communications weaves strength, continuity, and durability into our relationships. Difficult communications are transformed into positive outcomes. All communication is art precisely because there's no one way to do it. We grow our skills by trying, failing, and trying again. I often tell my students, "It is not what you do; it is what you do next."

PRACTICE

Receiving Feedback

1. Ask a close friend or colleague to give you constructive feedback. It helps to be specific like, "How do you think my work is going right now?" or "How are you experiencing me in relationship lately?"
2. Brace yourself. You'll be amazed how ready people are to offer their opinions.
3. Take a couple of even inhalations and exhalations, and notice any bodily resistance to the feedback. Let the resistance be there.
4. Simply listen and repeat what you have heard. Refrain from explaining or commenting in any other way on the feedback. Just feel what it is like to take it in.

PRACTICE

Giving Feedback

1. Wait for a situation to come up in which you would like to offer constructive feedback to a friend or colleague.
2. First, ask for their permission. They may not give it.
3. Begin with a sentence or two of appreciation.
4. Offer a simple observation that might serve them if they're receptive. An example might be, "I notice that when attention comes your way, you tend to move away from it." Or, "I would like it if you put your handheld away when we are eating."
5. Always follow the feedback with a question such as, "How do you feel about this?" or, "What is your experience of this?"
6. Say thanks for the opportunity to be open and real.

17

The Shadow in Conflict

Anyone who perceives his shadow and his light simultaneously
sees himself from two sides and thus gets in the middle.
CARL JUNG[1]

A FRIEND OF MINE went on a solo meditation retreat. The instructions were simple. She was to meditate in a small cabin for about eight hours a day. She was permitted to bring along two dharma books to read but told not to distract herself with other activities.

During one of the meditation breaks, my friend went outside for a short walk. As she walked in the forest, a piece of wood laying on the ground caught her eye. She picked it up and carried it back to the cabin, placing it on the altar. She continued to meditate like she was supposed to, admiring the natural beauty on her shrine.

As the day went on, the piece of wood began to change. Eyes appeared first, then a nose and mouth. More details emerged, until by the end of the day, a full-blown face peered back at my friend.

The next morning, during a break after the morning meditation, rather than reading dharma, my friend took the piece of wood outside again. She took out her pocket knife and started carving the face out of the wood. By this time, she saw that she was, indeed, involved in a distracting activity, but she couldn't stop herself.

The more my friend carved, the more menacing the face became. Where before it had been innocent, now it was ugly, with harsh gashes and scrapes from the knife. She put it back on her shrine anyway, curious about how the face was changing before her. She had gone from admiring a beautiful piece of wood on the shrine to seeing an innocent face peering out to confronting a mean, frightening face. The woody demon had begun to haunt the retreat cabin.

After her meditation period the next morning, she decided she had to remove the face from the piece of wood. It was just too strange and disturbing there on the altar. So she took the wood outside once more and made a rather odd choice. She tried to get rid of the face by burning it away. She used a cigarette lighter and, holding the wood over the flame, burned it until it turned black.

Then she went back into her hut and placed the burned piece of wood back on the altar. But instead of the face disappearing, now it had become even scarier. The ugly, sharp lines were charred, and all day long while she meditated, the burned, frightening face of the demon stared back at her like a dark deity in a Tibetan painting.

By the next morning's break, she felt she had to get rid of the piece of wood altogether. It didn't seem right to toss it back into the woods. She had created it, so it deserved a proper burial. So she went into the woods with the scary face, with which she now had a very intimate relationship. She dug a hole, dropped the demon into it, and buried it under a mound of dirt and dry leaves. The demon had come, and the demon had gone. It was a good thing, since it was the last day of her retreat.

In Jungian psychology, the shadow is the unconsciousness, or the darker aspects of the self of which we are unaware. These are the parts of ourselves that we disown, forget, project onto other people or pieces of wood, or bury. For Jung, then, the shadow refers to anything that lies outside the light of conscious awareness. "Everyone carries a shadow," he wrote, "and the less it is embodied in the individual's conscious life, the blacker and denser it is."[2]

For example, a friend sees herself as kind and supportive but makes sharp, cutting remarks without seeming to notice them. Ironically, she feels that others are often unkind to her. If you point out her aggression, she doesn't see it.

A perpetually upbeat friend seems sad, but when you inquire about it, she sees only the sadness in the world, and her virtuous desire is to cheer everyone up. Another friend disapproves of sexual desire during the day but at night has vivid, erotic encounters in his dreams. He speaks of his dreams as though they have nothing to do with him. A classic example of shadow is the religious zealot who fuels hatred for homosexuality while having private experiences in public restrooms.

From an Integral perspective, Ken Wilber would describe the shadow as any part of consciousness that we cannot acknowledge in first person as "I":

"I'm not angry. You are."

"I'm not unfaithful. She is."

"I'm not greedy. They are."

A shadow is a perspective that we refuse to take for all kinds of reasons; it is shameful, frightening, painful, or socially offensive. Whatever the reason, it is deeply unacceptable to our sense of self, and we cannot claim it. This split-off quality was once a part of our "I." But because it posed a threat to self-identity, it became unacceptable; it was pushed out of awareness and landed in second person, where it is projected onto others. I see it in you but not in me. You are stingy or impatient or lazy, while I am not.

When the threat of this emotion or trait becomes so great that it requires total rejection, we push it even further away from our awareness, banishing it to third person, to the status of "it" or "them" or "those people." From a third-person perspective, we disdain and judge the quality more intensely. We all know what can happen when one group of humans decides that another group is the source of all that is wrong in the world, and "they" become an "it." Collective shadow leads to war and genocide.

Wilber says that the discoveries of Freud, Jung, and their lineage were among the most important of the twentieth century. "If the negative qualities of someone else merely inform us, that is one thing," he explains, "but if they annoy, obsess, infuriate, and disturb, then chances are, we are caught in a serious case of shadow-boxing, pure and simple."[3] The psyche, and reality itself, has an innate intelligence that will keep presenting us with the material that we most need to look at but can't until we do the work.

It is imperative to own shadow, because ignoring it comes at a great cost. We expend precious life energy when we reject part of our identity and keep it hidden from our awareness. We develop rigidity, a phony quality, or an artificial air of goodness.

Our communications are often incongruent; our words are out of sync with our way of being. Our ability to be authentic and natural with others is inevitably compromised when we repress certain thoughts and feelings. Our inability to touch the places in ourselves that we fear and judge makes us critical and fearful of the world.

Shadow in Conflict

I learned about working with shadow in the trenches. As a group facilitator of difficult conversations, I often encountered hidden perspectives that people were unwilling to identify with or voice. We might be exploring racial bias, but nobody would claim the prejudice. A bigot was lurking in the back alley of the conversation, but he never appeared in the room or sat at the table with the rest of us.

In a divorce mediation, both parents would accuse the other of putting their own needs ahead of the children, but neither could acknowledge even once that they had been a neglectful parent. As they argued and bickered over every detail, they neglected the important issue of creating a plan to care for their children.

During mediations over business disputes, accusations of dishonest dealings or unfair practices dominated the conversation, but nobody ever saw themselves as unethical. How could that be? I wondered if it is possible to be truly ethical without acknowledging shadow.

I clarified my own experience with shadow when I trained with renowned group facilitator and author Arnold Mindell, a Jungian analyst and former faculty member at the Jungian Institute in Zurich who founded Process-Oriented Psychology. With his cofacilitator and partner, Amy, Arny would jump into the most harrowing of conversations and use his Jungian training to navigate and transform them.

He emphasized paying attention to what was at the forefront of our awareness while also noticing what was occurring around the edges of our experience. What were the unintentional body signals, marginalized voices, and unpopular ghostlike roles in the room? What were we dreaming about? What were people thinking or saying to others but unwilling to express to the group?

His questions always brought the shadow into the light, and he always treated the shadow voices with respect and compassion. He recognized the wisdom in these unpopular perspectives and affirmed the transformational power of shadow once it is reclaimed.

Signs of the Shadow

There are always signs when a shadow is present. Just as the unarmed citizens of a small town scatter when an outlaw rides into town, our discourse becomes chaotic and confusing when an unacceptable perspective rides into the conversation. We jump from one topic to another or recycle unproductively through the same topic. We whisper to each other or have conversations on the side. Our speech becomes agitated or overly heated. The room loses energy as abruptly as the endangered citizens start closing their shutters. The conversation stalls, and no progress is made. Even when there is progress, it feels like it won't stick.

When these signals come up, I pay attention to what isn't being said. As a facilitator, it is my job to bring the shadow voice into focus. But since nobody wants to identify with the voice directly, I often have to speak it myself, saying what nobody else wants to say. Sometimes these comments are politically incorrect, sometimes impolite, and almost always risky, but they can bring the room back to life, creating coherence and restoring flow.

An environmental coalition, which had just completed their first large-scale negotiation with the federal government in Washington, D.C., hired me to help them address the next step in their complex negotiations over wilderness designation. Although they were proud of their accomplishments in the first round, they seemed to lack energy and focus as we started to plan their strategy for the next round. Something didn't feel right. I suspected an unspoken conflict. Because the coalition consisted of like-minded groups, perhaps they feared alienating one another.

Several times, I probed them about the quality of their work relationships. How was everyone getting along? "Fine. No problem." The energy didn't change, so I decided to take a risk. I imagined myself in their position as an environmental advocate, but when I contemplated moving forward with their agenda, I felt like I was walking out onto a loose diving board. Something was going on that I didn't trust. I shared this with them, emphasizing the word *distrust*.

At first, they were offended and criticized my intervention. But gradually they started talking about their mistrust. They didn't trust the motives of the government and its ability to keep its word. They were disappointed in the inevitable competition and positioning that had arisen between organizations during high-stakes negotiations. Most important, they didn't have faith in their effectiveness as an environmental coalition.

Great doubt lurked in the background as to their level of competence and sophistication in this negotiation. It was their first complex land deal, and they questioned whether they had the skills to succeed. On the surface, they seemed confident, even brazen. But deep down, they were timid, halting, and unsure. They couldn't voice their distrust to each other, let alone themselves, for fear of weakening the coalition and compromising their goals.

Once the conversation opened up, everything changed. The room became more vivid, more alive. Energy started to flow. The conversation became more intimate, personal, and detailed; by including rather than ignoring the shadow of doubt, they shifted to a whole new level of strategic planning. That strategy now included ways to increase communication between them and strengthen their sense of teamwork. Their environmental zeal was tempered by pragmatism, and their idealism was balanced by the genuine challenges that lay ahead.

3-2-1 Integral Shadow

Shadow work is devoted to recovering those parts of ourselves that we have exiled or projected onto others. Once we recognize our shadows, we can reverse the process and bring them gradually back into awareness.

Ken Wilber and his team at the Integral Institute incorporated the three primary perspectives of first, second, and third person into a practice called 3-2-1. With each of these perspectives, we can access shadow qualities and integrate them into awareness. The 3-2-1 process is an enlightening practice to use in a conflict setting, because it helps us confront the parts of ourselves that we bring to a conflict but that we inevitably ascribe to the other side. By reconnecting with these disowned feelings and tendencies, we lower the boundaries between self and other, and we include our contribution to the struggle in our awareness.

Face It. The first step in the practice is to notice what is disturbing to us and to describe it in detail in third person. I once worked with a woman I will call LuLu in a workshop on shadow in a room of about two hundred people. She was a colorful character in her early sixties, wonderfully eccentric, with long, flowing gray hair and purple scarves. She was a natural performer with quirky charisma and a knack for being in front of an audience.

We sat face-to-face on the stage, and I asked her to describe her conflict with her landlord. She unloaded. "The landlady," she said, "is a terrible woman. She is untrustworthy, she is manipulative, and she lies. She's making my life impossible; I guess I'm going to have to move out of the apartment where I'm living."

"Wow," I said. "Sounds like trouble. There are a lot of negative qualities here. What do you like least about your landlady?"

Lulu paused for a moment, thought about it, and exclaimed, "She's a thief."

"She's a thief?" I said. I asked her what the woman had stolen.

Lulu went into a long story about her inheritance and bank accounts and how they had been emptied by the landlady. I was somewhat worried because I wasn't sure if we were in the territory of the real, but I decided to plow ahead.

Talk to It. So we took the next step in the practice together. We moved the unacceptable quality from the third-person perspective, "She is a thief," to the second person, "You are a thief." Bringing the quality from "she" to "you" moves it closer to our awareness. We can familiarize ourselves with the quality, ask questions, and get to know it more intimately.

In the exercise with Lulu, I stood in for the landlady, the thief, while Lulu asked me questions about what it is like to be a thief and why I steal. I did my best to find the thief in myself and explain it in first person. "As a thief, stealing is a very private affair. I am in need of something. It is there, available. I just need to take it. Nobody will know. I feel it belongs to me anyway, and I have no sense that anyone will be injured if I take it. As a thief, I steal more than things. I steal energy, attention, happiness."

Lulu seemed impressed with my access to my own thief. She asked me more about why I stole.

I went on, "I steal because I want more than I have. I steal because I deserve things, and I can't get them legitimately. I steal because I need the money now. I steal because I like the risk and the secrecy. I am compelled to take things, and I don't really know why, but I'm eyeing one of those scarves that you are wearing right now."

She laughed. She was getting great pleasure out of this exploration.

Be It. "Now," I asked Lulu, "are you ready to take the final step?" The third step is to find that very quality in yourself. So instead of "She is a thief," or "You are a thief," we shift the focus to "I" ("I am a thief"). So I asked Lulu to tell me about how she is a thief and steals from others.

Lulu looked flushed and a little dazed. She paused for a moment, reflecting, when someone yelled out from the audience, "You're stealing the show!" The entire audience broke into roaring laughter. Lulu began giggling, laughing, almost bubbling over. She had a brilliant, knowing smile on her face, and she said, "Oh my god, it's true. I am a thief."

"Really," I asked her, "how? What have you stolen?"

"I married my first husband for his money," she said, still giggling. "I emptied his bank account." Then she listed several other things she had stolen, including a pack of gum. Then the stealing became very serious. Forty years before, she had stolen a strand of pearls. She was never caught, and she had never told anyone until now. The intensity of her self-recognition as the thief of those pearls was very striking and poignant.

The session went from a victim's indignation to a confessor's catharsis. Everyone in the room was moved and couldn't wait to delve into their own shadows. Lulu remarked that her experience toward the landlady had completely altered in those few minutes. She understood that her long-standing and latent guilt had caused her to create situations in which she felt robbed. She had begun to integrate the identity of the one who steals rather than the one who is always in danger of being robbed.

The Gifts of Shadow Work

Shadow work, like the 3-2-1 process, brings unwanted aspects of the self back into wholeness. The energetic boundary between us and the projection dissolves, freeing up energy, as in Lulu's case. When the shadow quality is recognized as part of the self, people laugh and smile, their eyes light up with recognition, and sometimes they cry.

Almost immediately, compassion or empathy arises. The heart seems to soften, and the rough edges around the conflict melt. The accused person is no longer experienced as irritating, reprehensible, or bad and wrong. The weighty burden of judgment is dropped. At least for now.

Situations appear more workable. Other insights may emerge about how to approach the conflict differently. Once the projection is taken back, sometimes the conflict dissolves. Instead of being caught in a complex situation with someone or something we cannot control, we have pulled our focus back into the sphere of self where all of our creative energy resides.

It is not that our perceptions about people are incorrect; Lulu's landlady may be a real piece of work. And there is no problem with seeing people as they are and working directly with that truth. But when we engage with shadow work, we can release the disturbance to our well-being. The outrage and indignation subside; now we can work on the real issues. The conflicts may not go away, but we see them differently. When we embrace the unacceptable, a tremendous amount of expansion and compassion arises, because now we can identify with everything. Shadow work changes us and, therefore, our relationship to the world. When we include the shadow, everything is truly us.

PRACTICE

3-2-1 of Shadow

1. FACE IT

Select a conflict you're having with another person. In your journal, describe the conflict and the other party. Use third-person pronouns, such as *he, him, she, her, they,* and *their.*

This is your opportunity to explore your experience fully, particularly the most bothersome parts. Don't minimize the disturbance. Describe it as fully as possible. Exaggerate it. In this part of the exercise, you are welcome to blame, finger-point, criticize, and reprimand. Enjoy it.

Now identify the one trait or quality of the person that is the source of the conflict. Is it their arrogance, their powermongering, their selfishness, their lack of organization?

2. TALK TO IT

In your journal, dialogue with the person about the quality that most disturbs you. This time use second-person pronouns (*you* and *yours*). This is your opportunity to make relationship with the disturbance, so talk to it directly. You may ask questions such as, "Who or what are you?" "Where do you come from?" "What do you want from me?" "What do you need to tell me?" "What gift are you bringing me?" Then allow the disturbance to respond to you. Allow yourself to be surprised by what emerges in the dialogue.

3. BE IT

Write or speak in first person with pronouns like *I, me,* and *mine.* Find the disturbing quality in you and speak as it: "I'm angry because..." or, "I'm so arrogant that..." Identify fully with the quality, exploring how it manifests in your life. Be specific. Notice how owning the shadow changes your relationship to the person and the problem. Finally, ask yourself what the shadow quality has to offer when you include it as part of the self.

What is the gift?

18

Evolving Worldviews

Some things never change,
and some things will never be the same.
ANONYMOUS

ALL IN THE FAMILY was one of the most popular and ground-breaking shows in television history. An American sitcom that ran from 1971 through 1979, it revolved around the character of Archie Bunker—a working-class head of the household notorious for his conservative and patriotic rants, his racist and sexist complaining—and as a charming blowhard, he was one of the best. There was something lovable about the guy: he knew what he knew, he said what he thought, and he didn't apologize for any of it. He was more blustery than mean, but while he was sure of himself, there was no doubt he felt his power waning. And because he was a working-class character, I identified with his preoccupations with social rank.

Archie lived with his timid, hand-wringing wife, Edith; their progressive daughter, Gloria; and her long-haired husband, Mike. In sharp contrast to Archie, Gloria and Mike were countercultural liberals, champions of social and racial equality, women's lib, and the peace movement—all things sixties. They were open-minded and tolerant, even though Archie would complain that Mike's spine was as weak as his belly was soft.

Although all the characters lived under the same cramped roof, their views of the world were miles apart. Edith didn't appear to have her own viewpoint or a sense of self, apart from shuffling around trying to keep others happy. Archie railed all day long about his pet peeves, drawing particularly strong boundaries in his diatribes between "us" and "them," whereas Mike and Gloria didn't make the same sharp distinctions between groups and had a more kumbaya view of the world. Strangely, in Archie's worldview, Edith, Mike, and Gloria all turned out to be "them." Edith and Gloria were women, and Mike was Polish.

Archie's predicament was that he lived in a house filled with "others," and he suffered for it. The conflicts and arguments that erupted in every episode—especially those between Archie and Meathead (Archie's pet name for Mike)—were what made the show so funny, dynamic, and socially relevant for its time.

Turn on any cable news channel today, and you will hear the same arguments that Archie and Mike were having forty years ago, but without the irony or humor. Probably you have an uncle or aunt who resembles Archie, who watches Fox News religiously and voted for George W. Bush. You might have another relative like Mike or Gloria, who gives money to environmental and human rights groups, listens to National Public Radio, and shops at Whole Foods. The details change depending on the decade, but the underlying structures remain the same. The conflicts between the characters are due to differences in worldviews. In any conflict, we need to be aware of the worldviews at play, because while many things can be negotiated, worldviews cannot.

What Is a Worldview Anyway?

Worldviews comprise a whole set of perspectives that influence our interpretation of reality and filter our experience. Our worldviews make our decisions predictable and our actions consistent. They also link us with like-minded people, and these relationships and affiliations reinforce how we see things. However, since a worldview is fundamentally a lens through which we view reality, it can evolve over time. As our worldview evolves, so does our ability to take a perspective on that worldview. (For a complete discussion of this topic, please see Ken Wilber's books *The Atman Project* and *Up from Eden.*)

Within each worldview reside the criteria for what we consider real, important, and valuable. When we are young, we don't have a worldview because our experience is so limited. We are mostly concerned with our immediate environment: meeting our needs, pleasing our family, getting our schoolwork done, or avoiding the bully in the neighborhood.

As we become more aware of the world, our identity expands to include our neighborhood, town, or city. We adopt the values, speech, and dress of our family, school, favorite sports team or street gang, our religion and nation. We know who is "us" and who is "them," and we don't cross those boundaries. We form political opinions and associate with causes, organizations, and religious groups that support our worldview. We derive tremendous safety and a sense of belonging from our groups. As we grow older, some of us continue to identify with the groups of our family and culture of origin, while others stray outside those boundaries and, like Gloria and Mike, venture into new territory.

If we keep expanding our perspectives through study, travel, and encounters with people from other cultures, our worldview may expand beyond group identities and boundaries. We may begin to entertain the perspectives of *all human beings,* even those who are different from us. We may notice an increase in our sensitivity to other life forms; plants, mammals, birds, and fish all matter, and we may even regard the planet itself as a living being.

If we go even further, we may eventually open up to an even greater perspective that includes all sentient beings throughout space and time. Even though we don't know these perspectives firsthand, we willingly acknowledge their validity and therefore are open to learning about them.

Because of the strength of our convictions, arguing about worldviews quickly becomes frustrating and pointless. We suddenly hit an impasse, and there is no moving forward in the conversation. Our worldview gives us firm ground to stand on, and from where we stand, we are dumbfounded as to why the other side doesn't see things our way. The truth is so obvious. And yet the other person feels exactly the same way about us. That is why most of us would agree that we shouldn't talk about politics or religion at social gatherings; such conversations can ruin dinner and sometimes friendships.

Worldviews Change

While incredibly stabilizing, worldviews can grow and change. As Ken Wilber points out, there is a whole body of work from developmental researchers like Clare Graves, Abraham Maslow, Jean Gebser, Robert Kegan, and Susanne Cook-Greuter, which shows that humans can learn and evolve throughout adulthood. Not that we always do, mind you. Many adults find a comfortable way to live life exactly as they always have, without significant changes in philosophy, worldview, or religious practice.[1]

For others, something has to change—usually in the wake of a trauma, loss, illness, or divorce. A serious challenge can upset the status quo of our lives, and we can't move on without expanding or changing the way we see things. For instance, I couldn't resolve my questions about the deaths of seven friends in high school without taking a long journey beyond the religion and culture of my up-bringing.

Sometimes the shift occurs when we notice hypocrisy in our worldview. Jesus's injunction to love others unconditionally may raise questions about the exiling of gays and lesbians from our church.

Or maybe a contradiction in our own life experience gets us off the dime. In 1964 my husband, an insatiable reader of Ayn Rand, voted for Barry Goldwater. Four years later he voted at the other end of the spectrum—for Eldridge Cleaver. His perspective, which valued individualism above all, rotated 180 degrees. From my husband's new vantage point, he decided that society does, indeed, have obligations to people, especially to the disadvantaged. As he puts it, "Instead of seeing the weight of certain people on society, I started to see that society itself can be a crushing weight to many, especially when it is blind to the impacts of its policies on people."

Sometimes our worldview changes when we are drawn to something just over the horizon. In the early eighties, I moved to New York so I could experience the art and music scene on the Lower East Side. Then I moved to Boulder, Colorado, to study at Naropa and prepare for a career. After graduating, I moved to Seattle. My newborn son had Down syndrome, and because of his heart condition, he needed to live at sea level where there is more oxygen. I was very fortunate; unlike many young people around the world, I had the means to travel beyond the next valley.

Whatever the circumstance that changes our worldview, we usually have to be pushed or pulled out of our comfort zone. It helps if we have a mentor, boss, or new friend with a more appealing worldview than ours.

A worldview is more than an opinion; it is an entire gestalt of opinions that frames meaning. It is impossible to persuade another person to adopt a new worldview, certainly not in the course of a single argument or negotiation.

So how do we handle the conflicts that arise from fundamentally different ways of viewing reality?

Deep Structures

Our perspectives are shaped not only by our personal or psychological history but by our education and professional training. Political trends, religious teachings, and class distinctions also have an impact. Even the drugs we take and the movies we watch affect how we see the world. Conversely, how we see the world helps determine the drugs we take and the movies we watch. The list of influences goes on and on. Given this complexity, why do our morning talk shows confine themselves to two competing viewpoints? Can any of us be reduced to such a simple equation?

Ken Wilber and the developmental psychologists whose work he respects make the distinction between the surface features and deep structures of consciousness. Say you are a fundamentalist Christian, and I am a fundamentalist Muslim. On the surface, we seem to have nothing in common—at least not in our language, dress, rituals, or theology. Yet the deep structure of our consciousness is similar. We are both dualistic thinkers with a rigid definition of good and evil, right and wrong; we see in black and white rather than in shades of gray. We each believe in the superiority of our group; our God is the only true God. Like Archie Bunker, you don't have to be religious for this deep structure to hold.

Here is another example. You are a conscious capitalist, and I am a revolutionary socialist. On the surface, we have vastly different ideas about government, the economy, and our role as private citizens. Yet at a deeper level, our worldview is human-centered. We both believe in equality; we advocate for fair economic practices and sustainable environmental policies. Despite the differences in our surface features, we share the same values and the same ultimate goal of a peaceful, prosperous planet.

Researchers have described and categorized these deep structures somewhat differently. A user-friendly way to think about them is to divide them into four stages, or levels.

Egocentric Consciousness. Egocentric means that our view of the world is centered on the "I." In other words, we focus on our own needs and desires. Our deepest motivation is to secure personal safety, fulfillment, success, or self-realization on our own terms. While we tend to think of the label *self-centered* in less than favorable terms, it is a necessary step in development. Like many women in her shoes, Edith Bunker didn't seem to have much sense of a self. Without the ability to stand up for herself and state her wants, needs, and preferences, she was bound to become depressed or hapless. It might have done her some good to think more about her own wants and needs, but ironically, she needed support to do that.

A healthy sense of "I" is essential for self-care and personal development and integrity. When we honor our own dignity, we can recognize the same dignity in others. Thus, egocentric awareness forms the foundation for the more inclusive forms of awareness of ethno-, world-, and cosmic-centric consciousness.

A strong sense of "I" provides a basis for continuing to grow, but sometimes we don't. We all know people who do not have the ability to think about others, let alone care for them. They may neglect the needs of their own children because they're focused on securing themselves and satisfying their own needs, sometimes unsuccessfully. I remember a young friend in grade school whose dad was so involved in his sports activities that it was clear, even to someone as young as I was, that the father's obsession was more about his own sense of worth than his son's.

Highly egocentric types relate to others as if they are props in a play; if the people in their lives do not follow the script, they are of little use. The truth, however, is that when we can't take other people's interests into account, we end up isolated, hardened, and bereft of social support. Sometimes, due to injury, personality structure, addiction, or moral failing, people get stuck in the back eddy of their own narcissism.

When we do take the developmental leap and grow beyond the

egocentric stage, we don't leave the self behind. It remains an appropriate internal reference point, like a point on a compass, as our eyes take in the greater territory around us.

Ethnocentric Consciousness. The next step of this four-stage model is referred to as ethnocentric. This stage occurs when we learn to put the group's needs ahead of our own. The group could be our family, clan, or tribe; our nation or religious group; or even our team or company. Loyalty, teamwork, service, and self-sacrifice are virtues that emerge at the ethnocentric stage.

This stage of consciousness creates coherent, supportive communities that are stable and enduring. People attend each other's weddings and funerals. They know when babies are born, when kids graduate from high school, and the community lends a hand when someone is ill or dying. The quality of community—the safety, belonging, and identity it provides—is the crown jewel of ethnocentric consciousness.

To taste the full expression of ethnocentric energy, with all of its excitement, attend a football game. Two cultures come together precisely to clash, backed up by marching bands. Team colors, flag waving, and cheering support the competition and rivalry, which are at a full pitch. And even when he doesn't get to the game, someone like Archie Bunker is fully at home in his stadium living room, rooting for the home team and insulting the other side. This energy is fun when it is contained but can become extremely dangerous when it breaks out in the world at large.

The limitations of ethnocentric consciousness include black-and-white thinking, blind conformity, a rigid adherence to fixed moral codes and rules, and the strong division of the world into "us" versus "them." The cohesion of the community is fueled by a perceived threat from the outside, and there are always enemies at this level of consciousness. Most conflicts and wars result from the collision of ethnocentric groups, whether tribes, nations, or religious groups. Yet ethnocentric consciousness remains a powerful, inescapable source of social cohesion and meaning.

World-Centric Consciousness. We receive security, belonging, and a sense of safety at the ethnocentric stage, but it can, in our modern world, become suffocating. The conformity it demands negates the individual who questions, as well as the validity of other cultural perspectives. The dogma and pressure to conform that is comforting at one level of development becomes oppressive at another. Then a break occurs: leaving the town we grew up in, distancing ourselves from old friends or colleagues, or being discharged from the military in a surprising state of disillusionment as we ask far bigger questions than we did when we enlisted.

A move to world-centric consciousness may mean that we no longer distinguish between our side and the enemy's. As we begin, we recognize the same aspirations and suffering in ourselves and others, the whole enterprise of nationalism collapses in our mind. Biases based on national identity, race, or ethnicity have dissolved. In their place is a set of universal human values and a care that extends beyond our group to everyone.

Many world-centric people today easily take multiple perspectives on problems. They are interested in differences rather than afraid of them. They are often less religious, putting their faith in social, scientific, and technological innovations rather than religious dogma. They believe humanity can improve its lot more reliably through empiricism, science, and technology, thereby creating freedom, opportunity, and justice for all.

It is an expansive vision—and a good one—but very hard to realize on the ground, as anyone who has worked for a global humanitarian cause knows. Unless we continue to grow into even greater awareness as we work for the human good, the problems of the world become increasingly overwhelming to our world-centric views. Addressing the pervasive problems of poverty, human rights, labor and sex slavery, the arms trade, or HIV/AIDS will often provoke another developmental move. This shift, the one that addresses the Great Matter of Life and Death, begins to prevail over the serious but relative concerns of the world. These concerns begin to be held in the vast space of cosmic-centric contemplation.

Cosmic-Centric Consciousness. The word *cosmos* refers both to the physical universe and to consciousness itself. Cosmic-centric consciousness is vast, boundless, and all-inclusive. It exists in the realm of time, yet it is beyond it. It takes form but is formless. It permeates all things, animate and inanimate alike, but is beyond the duality of existence and nonexistence. This vast consciousness is not limited to the reasoning mind; in fact, it is unlimited, ungraspable, and unknowable. At this level of consciousness (here, the word *level* begins to lose meaning), all distinctions of the conceptual mind cease to exist in their customary form. Talking about it, we might question its value. But as we relax the demands and categories of the reasoning mind and begin to recognize the deep reality of Being itself, our doubts fade. Sometimes we use the expression "Unity consciousness" to describe the vast presence of which we are all wholly a part. Some call it Love; others, God.

The mystic poets convey this reality beautifully. Rumi, a Sufi, says, "Again I am stunned by the grandeur of the unseen One that governs all movement."[2] The Christian saint Teresa of Avila asks, "What are these different names for the same church of love we all kneel in together?... And God is always there, if you feel wounded. He kneels over this earth like a divine medic, and His love thaws the holy in us."[3]

From this perspective, the challenges of the world no longer seem overwhelming or insurmountable. Indeed, every spiritual tradition promises that when enlightenment is attained, God is realized, or the human heart opens to its grandest proportion, the world itself ceases to be seen as a problem. Rather, we are oriented to love, to serve, and to appreciate. All of our challenges are part of the path, and as Chögyam Trungpa has said, "Everything is workable."

People with a cosmic-centered perspective are truly, as Christ said, "in the world, but not of it." Their very presence manifests this paradox. They transcend yet include the other levels in their lives and work. His Holiness the Dalai Lama champions the cause of the Tibetans while also teaching people of all faiths across the globe. Even while he struggles on behalf of Tibet, he also recognizes the inherent value and beauty of all sentient beings—even the Chinese, who, from an ethnocentric perspective, are the oppressors of his own people. Cosmic-centric consciousness includes the ego-, ethno-, and world-centric realms. Each level belongs to itself and is contained and pervaded by the infinite whole.

Can't We All Just Get Along?

We will never be surrounded by people with similar worldviews. The boundaries of our egos will forever run into other egos; cultures will scrape against other cultures as they always have, and creative friction will spark as part of humanity's movement through time and evolution. Those with world-centric consciousness may learn to work more harmoniously together, without the ethnocentric conflicts, but they will—at least for now—collide with mortality, disease, shrinking space, and the limited resources of the Earth. Diversity is the ultimate expression of our unity. Thank goodness. We really don't want to live in a global cult. We appreciate both the unity of reality and the diversity of the world.

When we recognize the validity of differing worldviews, we can take pleasure in listening to, seeing, and understanding others without asking them to change. We can suspend our tendency to assume that if only we could convince them, they *would* see reality the way we do.

To genuinely respect the perspectives of others, we must first come to know each level in ourselves. The nature of having views is that we conflate them with reality. But when we can stand back and look at the filter of our own worldview rather than through it, we have reached a bright line of development. Then we can begin to challenge our assumptions instead of everyone else's. In other words, to be able to take a "perspective on our perspective" is one way of describing what it means to be conscious.

We can observe the egocentric self, seeing how it plays out, and give it a rest. We can experience our ethnic identity swelling with pride or shrinking with shame, and instead of protecting ourselves or attacking, we can wait in the open space of awareness for things to calm down. We can taste the immensity of hope of the world-centric perspective without being overwhelmed with dread and panic. And we can revel in the sublime recognition of our spiritual nature as we work tirelessly on behalf of a particular cause, refreshed and fulfilled as we are compelled to the wisest and most compassionate action. Each level of consciousness has its own spiritual expression for, indeed, we are all one.

At the cosmic-centric level of consciousness, we become curious about how each level expresses itself in our life. We can be quick to recognize the limitations and the gifts of each level, and although we may vehemently disagree with Archie Bunker or our Republican uncle's political beliefs, we can acknowledge his worldview, which has its own validity and goodness.

We don't have to change anyone's worldview; we have to work with it. Each of us grows and develops in our own mysterious way, and we are complete whether we peer through an egocentric, ethnocentric, or world-centric lens or experience the lens as it dissolves altogether. Once we grasp the importance of developmental levels, we cultivate a boundless open space for all worldviews to be present while privileging those that take the most into account. In some real sense, we have to accept that we *can't* all just get along—at least not yet.

PRACTICE

Evolving Worldviews

Explore each level of identity by completing the following sentences:

As the egocentric self, I am aware of _____.
As the egocentric self, I am afraid of _____.
As the egocentric self, I aspire to _____.

As the ethnocentric self, I am aware of _____ in my culture.
As the ethnocentric self, I am proud of _____ in my culture.
As the ethnocentric self, I am ashamed of _____ in my culture.

As the world-centric self, I am aware of _____.
As the world-centric self, I am hopeful _____.
As the world-centric self, I am afraid of _____.

As the cosmic-centric self, I am aware of _____.
As the cosmic-centric self, I am aware of _____.
As the cosmic-centric self, I am aware of _____.

19

The Compassionate Heart

One must love everything.

VIRGINIA WOLFE[1]

JERI AND I HADN'T SPOKEN for a year. It had been a classic girl-friend falling out. She had moved from Utah to the Pacific North-west, and we weren't connecting by phone very often. I was working a new job that demanded my attention, and I was probably less avail-able than I had been before.

She had become much closer to Randee, a mutual friend of ours, through their frequent phone calls. This resulted in a bit of jealousy and awkward triangling between the three of us, as well as some mis-understanding. Matters were complicated by the fact that Jeri had a new boyfriend who I didn't like much. Add a dose of friendship fatigue that sets in over ten or fifteen years, and there you have it: the perfect recipe for a falling out. I guess something needed to shift be-tween us, and when we couldn't find a way to talk it through, we just quit talking. Maybe you have been through something similar. (As is often the case, no one was really to blame, but it felt like she was).

Suddenly, after a year of us not speaking, she was back in Salt Lake for the weekend. She called me and said, "Let's put up the dogs and have a drink."

"Well, uh, sure, of course," I said. Her invitations were always hard to resist; I loved her unconventional approach to things. But after I hung up, I experienced a rush of hurt and vulnerability that I couldn't sort through. I wanted to get together, but at the same time, I didn't want to touch back into the pain of our estrangement. I assumed it would be awkward between us, and when I tried to imagine talking over the past year, my mind quit. There was no sense in trying to go over it or talk it through. So I sat there bewildered. *What do I do?*

I looked over at the large statue of Kanzeon Bodhisattva sitting on my dresser. Kanzeon is the Goddess of Compassion in the Buddhist tradition; in China she is sometimes known as Kuan Yin. Her name means the "One Who Hears the Cries of the World," and she represents the enduring presence of compassion in spiritual life. She is relaxed, sitting in what is called the posture of Royal Ease. She wears loose-fitting garb. Jewels enhance her neck and wrists, and her hair is pulled up into a knot on her head. Her legs are slightly open; one knee is propped up, and her arm dangles over it, casual and sensual. But her spine is straight, and so is her gaze. She is supremely at home in herself, present to all that is and deeply awake to all that is beyond form. I had given her a large feather to hold in one hand and a beaded medicine bag to wear. I had also placed a small ceramic owl on one of her shoulders because of my love of birds.

I had never made a request to a goddess before, since I only related to them as symbols. But suddenly, looking at her on my dresser, I spontaneously spoke to her: "I am just going to give this evening to you, Kanzeon, because I don't know how to navigate my conflicting feelings, and I know you are wise in the ways of these things."

I sprang up, inspired to take the two-foot statue outside to the garden. I placed a woven piece of Guatemalan fabric in the middle of a small patio table and set her on top of it. Then I put six or seven glass votive candles in front of her and lit each one. By now my anxiety was gone, and I was in a mood of complete aesthetic enjoyment. I went back inside to get a bottle of wine and glasses, flowers, and a plate of fresh peaches, cucumbers, and tomatoes for my guest.

In the meantime, Randee, the other member of this complicated triangle, called. She knew Jeri was in town and that we were getting together. She wanted to come over. I thought to myself, *No way. I can handle one of them, but together, these girls are too much.* I paused, and again my mind seemed to fall off a shelf. I couldn't say yes, and I couldn't say no. So I said, "All right."

Soon after, Amy, another friend I hadn't seen for months, called. It was strange that she contacted me that same evening. A few years before, we had socialized often, but since she had left for medical school, I hadn't seen her for some time. When she heard the others were on their way, she said she was coming too. A little while later, she was walking up the winding steps to my front door in the mellowing golden light of a Utah summer evening, looking like a living goddess with her dark skin, broad bare shoulders, and sensual hips wrapped in a summer sarong. I welcomed her in.

Soon all four of us were sitting outside in my small, enclosed garden, sipping wine together. Jeri was tenderly fingering the pages of a book of Edward Curtis's Native American portraits, dove-cooing over their sepia beauty. Randee held a pocket mirror up to her face, smiling as she outlined her sculpted lips in her favorite matte red lipstick. Amy sat happily in summer sandals with painted bronze toenails, and Kanzeon was silent, gracing us with her ineffable presence. All was right with the world. We sat the whole evening together without speaking about the past. It was completely unnecessary in the power of the beautiful present. Thank goodness for the here and now. I simply felt grateful for this brand-new moment and fully compassionate toward everything we had been through. I didn't say a word; speaking about the past was unnecessary.

Compassion

For anyone working with conflict, *compassion* is a core capacity. What is compassion? I would say that it is the expression of our empathy toward one another, our ability to feel tenderness for ourselves and a suffering world. "It is to extend our heart," as Virginia Wolfe says, "to loving everything."[2]

Our conceptual mind is often unable to resolve life's most compelling questions; for example, why are we born, and why do we die? Why do we suffer or have to witness the suffering of people we love? Why can't we talk to an old friend like we used to, without tension or misunderstanding?

What the mind can't reconcile, the heart does. It metabolizes our pain, transforms our grief, and integrates all that is unacceptable to us. Compassion flows from a heart that brings nonjudgmental presence to the inevitable pain and conflicts of being human. Inevitably, our relationships will fail us, our communications will become disastrous, and our negotiations will break down. At these times, surrendering our preferences to the Great Heart, or Big Heart, of What Is, or any other purveyor of unbounded compassion, allows us to embrace the unsolved and unanswerable in our own experience.

Small Compassion versus Big Heart

The compassion of the ego is small. How could it be otherwise? When we look into it closely, we see that our compassion is often based on the motivations of the small self. We want to be noticed, appreciated, reimbursed, or at least be seen as a nice, caring person. Often, in the face of someone else's pain, our compassion is mixed with pity or distress, and we offer comfort to make ourselves feel better. Sometimes our expression of compassion is a way of saying, "Don't hit me," like Rodney King did to the Los Angeles police. It's part of an unspoken contract to take it easy on each other. Perhaps we are compassionate because we think we should be, because that's what our parents taught us, so we dutifully add compassionate acts to our to-do list and check them off.

The cool thing about real compassion is that, if this is indeed our motivation, we can be compassionate toward ourselves about that.

The compassion that arises from our meditation practice is different. It stems from our willingness to see things as they are rather than as we would like them to be. Instead of being conjured up and dutifully delivered, it rises from the direct truth of circumstances as naturally as mist from a grassy plain in the new light of morning.

Some say this natural compassion is built into the hard drive of our species because it supports our survival in small groups. Others say that it is intrinsic to the universe itself; reality is, finally, a great kindness when our hearts and minds are clear enough to experience it as such. Some believe that our compassion is a reflection of God's essential nature, and our spiritual task is to aspire to this divine quality.

From a Buddhist point of view, compassion arises free of references to the small self. Compassion takes many forms and perfectly complements the suffering of a world that expresses itself not in oppositional but in complementary pairs. Without suffering, there can be no compassion, and without compassion, there can be no suffering. Each depends on the other to exist, and our recognition of the interdependent nature of these opposites reveals the ultimate whole.

Discovering Big Heart

Without sustained practice, we habitually contract and defend against pain. With practice, we learn to identify with the space surrounding all pain. This is the open, boundless presence of Big Mind. Soon we see that it includes Big Heart as well. Our compassion, our patience, and our generosity arise from the deep acceptance of things as they are.

Freed from the compulsion to make things better for our own comfort, we can see clearly. From our awakened view, we are impartial (not indifferent; there is a profound distinction) toward this world. This very impartiality enables us to care profoundly. We can feel tender, poignant, and protective toward all things in creation, allowing them, too, to be as they are. Paradoxically it seems, we are more immediately helpful, without the attachments of the ego to gratifying outcomes.

The Chinese word *shin* means heart and mind. When we identify with Big Heart, we discover that, like the unbounded space of Big Mind, we can feel everything: the raw pain of conflict or loss; our railing against it; our failed attempts to fix it; and equally, our success in resolving conflict or relieving suffering. Every nuance of experience is included; thus we arrive at the transcendent form of compassion for ourselves and, therefore, for all.

Master Dogen says, "When one sees an exhausted turtle or an ailing sparrow, one doesn't want their thanks—one is simply moved to helpful action."[3] Our hands become willing vehicles of these actions, but we don't call them "mine." They belong to compassion itself. We are spontaneously generous, without the limits and conditions that constrain our smaller identities. The distinction between serving and being served blurs, and we forget to keep accurate accounts. As Hafiz says, "Look what happens with a love like that. It lights the whole sky."[4]

Hurt, Disappointment, and Grief

We might as well get used to it. Short of living on permanent retreat alone, we are bound to experience difficult feelings in relationship. The moment these strong responses occur, they don't feel fleeting, empty, or illusory. Rather, they constitute the deep, instinctive response of the body as it tries to protect itself. Jealousy, grief, anger, and betrayal can be so strong that we may fear we will never feel good again. In the aftermath of the death of a spouse, the betrayal of a lover, or a falling out with a friend or business partner, there's no circumventing these feelings; they must be lived through, or we risk becoming estranged from our own bodies.

There is a beautiful story of a Tibetan master who cried when his child was killed. His students protested, "Don't cry," because he had taught that reality is an illusion. The master told them that losing a child is the greatest illusion. And a father needs to cry when a child dies.

Willingness to Feel

When we are held captive by strong emotions such as rage, jealousy, or grief, we can work with them by giving in to them instead of resisting or bypassing them. Forget your sitting posture; lie down for a while and let the body metabolize the experience that the mind resists. This surrender to sensation may feel extremely bad; often we are deeply conditioned to keep the lid on our grief, but the heart and body know what they're doing.

Surrendering to unwanted sensations is itself a form of compassion. Our heart demands to be felt. As we weep, yelping or howling perhaps, our bodies soften, our nervous system reorganizes and adapts, and we move on, like a child after a bout of tears.

But before we can give in, let go, and relinquish to the wisdom of the body, we must drop the cherished stories running through our minds: stories about how this shouldn't be happening to us, about the wrongheadedness of the other, about how unfair life is. Any attachment to the thoughts that protest our feelings will prevent the body from doing what it knows how to do.

We may resist grief for fear of drowning in it. With anger or jealousy, we may be terrified that we will burn up. But we won't. We will just feel. Feelings roll through like great storms. Soon we learn not to be afraid of them but to relax into them as they rise up and pass away. Grief passes over us like a wave, then recedes, and like the calm after the storm, the space of Big Heart opens. We feel tenderness in our heart and the kind breath of compassion itself.

When we allow the body to do its job without protest, grief can be transformed into praise, anger into clarity, jealousy into freedom.

Finally, when dealing with hurt, it is good to remember that it always cuts both ways. Even as we are hurt, we are bound to inflict injury. We are both oppressor and oppressed, perpetrator as well as victim. While we are certain to be hurt in love, we are equally certain to hurt others. Nobody escapes unscathed. So forgiveness isn't an option: it is an essential. As compassion is to suffering, forgiveness is to injury.

Our spiritual work shows us that pain is endlessly woven into the ever-changing fabric of being. We all hurt. We may not have the power to prevent or resolve all conflict, but we all have the power to transmute our suffering into compassion for ourselves and others. Sometimes this is our only option.

Working with our feelings, keeping our hearts open, and staying the compassionate course promote fearlessness and courage. As our awareness expands, we can guide ourselves into our most difficult experiences with openness and curiosity, available to new possibilities even when our options seem limited. Sometimes we just have to give up and let the Big Heart of Compassion take the reins.

PRACTICE

Compassionate Feeling

1. When you are overcome by a strong emotion, practice surrendering to it.
2. Take a comfortable physical posture and allow yourself to feel the texture of the sensations.
3. Notice any resistance to feeling, and meet it with an even breath.
4. Notice what stories you are telling yourself. Suspend all stories about the pain, and instead, just feel.
5. Where precisely does it hurt? What are the qualities? How do they shift and change?
6. Practice opening to the pain, breathing, and being fully present to it.

7. Allow all bodily responses to arise spontaneously, especially crying, writhing, or loud noises.

8. When you are done, feel the tenderness in your heart, the open space, and when you are ready, without your story, move on.

20

Expanding the Heart

Tell me what you care about, and I'll tell you how big you are.

UNKNOWN

LOVE HURTS, like the song says. The seventies rock band Nazareth made the song famous on the pop charts, but the incomparable Roy Orbison sang it best. Roy was a genuine musical alchemist, who consistently transformed pain into love. He sang delicately and sweetly about longing, loss, grief, and unrequited love. Inevitably, his songs begin with a tender lament, then build, rising through the complexity of his melodies and gaining power from his extraordinary four-octave range, until by the operatic endings, his lament is exalted into praise.

When I think about some of the details of Roy Orbison's life, my heart breaks. Like most artists, he was an extraordinarily sensitive soul. While enduring the ups and downs of his fame (he opened for the Beatles) and a demanding career on the road, he lost the love of his life, Claudette, in a motorcycle accident. Then his two eldest sons died in a fire that burned down his house while he was on tour. Devastated, he sold the property to Johnny Cash, who built an orchard on it.

Roy Orbison died at fifty-two. Still revered for his sublime voice, he is an icon of the tender and broken heart.

Compassionate Exchange

Listening to Roy Orbison, or a great blues singer like B. B. King or Billie Holiday, or the Reverend Al Green as he belts out an old-style gospel tune, we see that severe heartbreak can be transformed into beauty through music. Indeed, some say this is the function of all art. Laughter can do the same thing. And so can meditation.

Tonglen is a heart-based practice from Tibetan Buddhism that I learned while I was at Naropa Institute. The practice shows us how to feel into our pain and transmute it into great compassion. It is a practice often taught by Pema Chödrön, a student of Chögyam Trunpga Rinpoche and an inspiring Buddhist teacher in her own right.

You can think of tonglen as one of Roy Orbison's songs. We begin the practice modestly at first, confessing our own pain, feeling the texture of it, and end with compassion that includes all of life. The practice moves us through the increasing scales of me, you, us, and all of us.

Step One: Flashing on Open Space. Pema teaches that tonglen has four distinct stages.[1] The first stage is to simply flash on absolute *bodhichitta,* our awakened heart. We are intentionally opening to the stillness, silence, and space that is always present, such as what we may experience gazing out at the ocean or up at a starry sky late at night. There is no limit to this openness, no conditions on the expanse of space or inherent beauty of reality. This initial flash gives us confidence in the constant availability of our open heart.

Step Two: Feeling the Texture. In the second stage of tonglen, we work with the texture of suffering. Breathing in, we take in qualities that are dark and heavy. Breathing out, we send out qualities of light, coolness, and spaciousness. The heaviness is the real thing. We have all felt it. It is the claustrophobic quality of egoistic fixation, when we cling to our narrow views, our entrenched preferences, and negative thoughts. When we become angry, threatened, or jealous, our mind state immediately becomes hot, cramped, and extremely uncomfortable. Pema calls this the texture of poison, of neurosis or fixation.

On the other hand, when our attention is drawn away from egoistic patterns, the oppression lifts. You may also have noticed times when you are caught in your own drama and then something grabs your attention, and suddenly, your awareness is freed. Perhaps you have experienced a similar shift with your mother. One minute she is in a shit-bad mood, then she picks up the phone and says hello in a perfectly gracious tone. The funny part is that she is not faking it. Her hello comes from the part of her that is not fixated on herself; it is open, immediate, and available. Believe it or not, that is how flexible the mind is. "Hello." The shift is easy when we want to make it. Pema describes the texture of this openness as light, white, fresh, clear, and cool.

So in the second stage of tonglen, we work with textures. Breathe in black, heavy, hot light through every pore of your body, then radiate out white and cool light, also through the pores of your body, front and back, 360 degrees. Work with the two textures until they're synchronized; black is coming in and white is going out through the medium of the breath—in and out, in and out, in and out.

Sometimes when practicing, we may notice a bias toward one texture or the other. At times, we can easily breathe in the dark, heavy texture, and we don't want to let it go. This clinging mirrors the perverse way we derive comfort from our suffering, holding tight to it like a baby to a worn-out blanket, unwilling to shift our attention to the great space outside ourselves. Other times, the reverse is true. We have trouble taking the breath in, as if we will drown in its heaviness, so we skip quickly over the breath, readily releasing it in exchange for the relief of the exhalation and feeling of light.

Tonglen is an exercise in cultivating an unbiased attitude toward the difficulty of existence as well as its fundamental freedom, light, and openness. We are not mired in our suffering, nor do we demand that everything and everyone feel good all the time, walking about like members of the spiritual country club, pleased as punch with our status. Tonglen prevents the human tendency to either bypass the human struggle or become pious, as though we have actually accomplished something.

Step Three: Working with Particulars. The third stage of tonglen is working with a specific person who is suffering. It is a good idea to begin with ourselves. On the in-breath, we might take in qualities of self-recrimination, shame, or disappointment in ourselves. We might feel the contraction of being misunderstood, insufficient, or overwhelmed by a world that is moving rapidly beyond our control. Then we breathe out tenderness, sympathy, and self-love, releasing the cramped space of ego to the expansive openness of the heart.

Next, we breathe in the pain of a specific person: a friend, brother, or animal we wish to help. We breathe out spaciousness or kindness to that person. Pema suggests offering them "a good meal or a cup of coffee—whatever we feel would lighten their load."[2]

This is another stage in the practice during which we may experience a bias. It may be easier to do the practice for ourselves than for others. Or it may be easier to do the practice for others than to focus on ourselves. We can notice this lopsidedness, be curious about it, and continue cultivating an attitude of impartiality toward ourselves and others.

There are people in my own life whose personal heartbreak seems greater than my own, so much so that I hesitate to contemplate it. I resist out of respect for them, out of the recognition that I can never really know what they have endured. My own father lost his two brothers, mother, father, and oldest sister by the time he was thirteen. That left him and his remaining two sisters to grow to adulthood alone. I have no way to imagine how he navigated the difficulty of those deaths. And like a veteran of war (which he was), he never cared to talk much about it.

All of the spiritual traditions teach us to include the suffering of others in our thoughts and to pray for their health and well-being. Occasionally, this practice has made me somewhat self-conscious. I subject myself to a negative image of a bleeding heart raised in relative comfort who identifies with another person's suffering in order to give my own life substance. Bringing the image of others into the practice has felt almost sacrilegious, pretentious, or an invasion of the privacy of another's unique path, spectating while they actually had to walk it.

Nonetheless, I have seen that the spiritual traditions are right. As humans, we are nourished by our ability to love, and we are enhanced by our empathy and care for others. As I have reflected on my father's childhood experiences, I have gotten to know him more intimately. I have shared his memory of seeing his mother die of cancer at the age of ten; experiencing his father's death at the age of twelve; and learning at age thirteen that his twenty-nine-year-old sister, whom he had gone to live with, had just died on the operating table as her tonsils were removed.

Contemplating the losses of my father's early life, as well as my mother's family's struggles with poverty and alcoholism, has always been a swinging door for me into greater contemplations of the suffering of all beings. My attention naturally moves from the personal and familial to the collective. I have found myself reflecting deeply on the decimation of Native culture in the American West where I grew up, wondering how anyone survived that genocide. I have considered the inhumane imprisonment of thousands of innocent Japanese at the Topaz internment camp near my family's home during the Second World War.

My uncle, now ninety years old, helped to build Topaz when he was just nineteen. The skeletal remains of the camp lay right next to what is left of my great-grandfather's meager farm. Life on his farm was no picnic, as extreme poverty and early death marked that desolate landscape in rural Utah. These reflections have become part of my practice, and they teach me to face suffering: my own and others.

I have learned to respect how much people have endured and how much, in this moment, people are going through.

Step Four: Contemplating the Universal. In the fourth stage of tonglen, we move from the specific to the general, from the personal to the collective, and from the particular to the universal. We now extend our wish to relieve the suffering of our spouse, parent, or friend to all people who are undergoing something similar, such as the loss of a loved one or the trauma of losing one's entire way of life. In this stage, we use specific instances of suffering as a stepping-stone to regarding the universal suffering of beings everywhere. As before, on our out-breath, we send out great love, spaciousness, and images of what would be healing to all.

Pema emphasizes that we need to work with both the third and fourth stages, beginning with the immediate suffering of one particular person or those in our intimate circle and expanding outward to include the suffering of other cultures and the universal suffering of all beings everywhere. The particular brings vividness and reality to the practice; the universal expands our vision and sense of the whole.

The Evolving Heart

The gradual progression in tonglen practice from a focus on ourselves, to those close to us, to the larger collective, and finally to the universal reflects the precise way in which our consciousness grows according to adult developmental psychology. From a developmental point of view, as our perspectives widen, so do our care and compassion.

As we explored earlier, we evolve from an egocentric orientation that values and protects only our own interests (we all know people who are limited to this) to an ethnocentric awareness that includes our families, groups, and people who think and act like we do. Under the right conditions, that perspective expands again so the boundary between "us" and "them" widens to encircle those who aren't our intimates or members of our community. We have moved to a world-centric perspective that doesn't draw ethnic and nationalistic lines but includes people of every culture, the great earth, and all forms of life: animals, insects, birds, and even plants.

Finally, there is no limit to our identity. We discover a cosmic-centric perspective in which form and formlessness, time and space, and the inevitability of joy and suffering are intrinsic to us. We are an inseparable part of a cosmos that is inevitably creative and destructive—both sides, like the inhalation and the exhalation. We are it. And so is everyone else.

Conflict work happens on all these levels. Our focus may differ at times in our lives: sometimes our work is the internal work of therapy or meditation; sometimes we engage the world with social work, conflict resolution, or diplomatic skills. All of this serves to transform the challenge of being human into compassionate action.

For example, working on the egocentric level in order to heal injuries from earlier life experiences helps us to quiet our internal conflicts and find peace and joy within ourselves. Some of this work is therapeutic; some of it, meditative. We may also choose to strengthen ourselves through athletics, expand one of our talents, or learn how to manage our money better. These activities enhance our self-esteem, and I would argue that a healthy ego is easier to relinquish than a shaky one.

At an ethnocentric level, we find ways to acknowledge the suffering of our own people and accept that we have inherited injuries from the past. We see how our mother's pain ends up in our own bodies and how our father's life crises are mirrored in our own.

Because of our direct experience with our line of ancestors, we come to see our own life in continuity with theirs. We don't have to do much, except to see them clearly, appreciating their lives and struggles while recognizing their limits and errors. Rather than being stuck in an unconscious back alley of our familial history, we learn to transcend and include it, valuing the pain and beauty of our whole ancestral line and our immediate family in the here and now.

In some of the groups I have worked with, people with world-centric points of view have rejected the traditions of their family of origin. In order to grow, they have relinquished any identification with the past. They don't want to be saddled with the dysfunction of their ethnic or national identity. They see themselves as world citizens and refuse to be affected by the historical dramas of the past.

But healthy development always includes integration. I remind them that without our ability to reintegrate our culture and history, we forfeit intense familial loyalty and cultural pride, and we lose a sense of belonging to the unfolding of generations. When it comes to dealing with the challenges of ethnic and nationalistic strife, we are handicapped, because we don't want to find that kind of bigotry inside of us. But it is there—everything is—and we are much more effective in our work when we can consciously acknowledge the presence and impact of it on our behavior.

As our awareness develops beyond limited identifications, we step into world-centric and cosmic-centric perspectives; we find ourselves increasingly turning toward conflict with curiosity and inquiry. We have learned to see it as part of the developmental unfolding of our lives and in that of the collective. Evolution is a messy business, but we are evolving in consciousness nonetheless. An open heart is capable of flowing with change, trusting, and relaxing in the face of complexity and challenges that feel overwhelming. This heart includes conflict and paradox, has infinite patience and faith in the unfolding, and doesn't mind the presence of a struggle.

The global crises of our times are challenging us to grow our hearts—from egocentric to ethnocentric to world-centric and, finally, to cosmic-centric levels of awareness and action. Remember that healthy development can't miss a stage, and it must transcend and include the previous level. Consciousness builds and expands like a Roy Orbison song, each level encompassing more of reality—including the pain—and transforming it into beauty.

PRACTICE

Compassionate Exchange

1. As in the practice of tonglen, flash on the awakened heart and feel the space, which is large enough to hold everything.

2. Relate with the texture of conflict, breathing in qualities of hot, dark, and heavy, and breathing out light, spacious, and cool. Do this for five minutes until the in- and out-breaths are synchronized. Be patient. It takes some practice.

3. Now reflect on a conflict in your life. Take your own side. Breathe in the challenging feelings of anger, hurt, or powerlessness. On the out-breath, free yourself completely, sending out compassion, self-love, and space. Do this for five minutes.

4. This time, expand to an ethnocentric level, and take in the heaviness of the conflicts of friends or loved ones. Breathe in their challenges, feel the difficult energy and emotions for them. On the out-breath, release the difficult sensations to wide-open space, light and free. Practice at this level for five minutes.

5. Now expand your circle of care to a world-centric level. Feel for places in the world where there is conflict or war. Take in the suffering of groups of people—people experiencing civil war in the Sudan or Afghanistan or a natural disaster—on the in-breath.

   Relate with their suffering on the in-breath, and on the out-breath, send them something to comfort them—a peaceful night's sleep, a good meal.

6. The last step takes you to a cosmic-centric level. On the inhalation, relate to the suffering that comes from being in form and the inevitable pain that all beings experience. On the exhalation connect again to tremendous space and compassion, a heart that is boundless, large enough to include everything. Practice this for five minutes.

21

Great Rivalry, Great Intimacy

I have been up against tough competition all my life.
I wouldn't know how to get along without it.
WALT DISNEY[1]

IN ALL OF OUR RELATIONSHIPS, there will be moments when we
oppose each other—unless we have the misfortune of being so seam-
lessly compatible that there is no creative tension, or we're in a relationship with such strict role definitions that we never step on each
other's toes. Optimally, opposition can be enlivening, contention can
be sexy, and both parties can stay aware of each other by jumping into
the rough patches.

If you don't know how to do this and are currently mired in
smoldering resentments, passive-aggressive tactics, or sulky withdrawal, take heart. You can learn how to enter the fray with another,
tolerate increasing levels of intensity, and get to know the precise

anatomy of your differences—all of which create authenticity and therefore deepen your intimacy in a sustained way.

A great poet once said that our lovers should be our worthy opponents. Great rivalries form the basis of sports, but they also fuel movements in art, science, and most fields of human endeavor. Queen Elizabeth and Mary Queen of Scots, Amadeus Mozart and Antonio Salieri, Henri Matisse and Pablo Picasso come to mind. Also Muhammad Ali and Joe Frazier; Steve Jobs and Bill Gates; Martina Navratilova and Chris Evert. Each duo had a vigorous and generative rivalry. Each was challenged, honed, and even in some sense completed by the existence of the other.

Martina and Chrissie ruled women's professional tennis in the seventies and eighties, and some would say theirs was one of history's greatest athletic rivalries. They formally played each other eighty times in sixteen years, but they also practiced together and teamed up in countless doubles matches. It is said they once shared a bagel while waiting to play for the U.S. Open title. These two women athletes had an uncommon friendship and the rarest intimacy in a context of intense competition. There were times when the competition strained the friendliness between them, but all these years later, they consider one another the best of friends precisely because of their rivalry. Their example can help us expand our notion of intimacy to see how challenges are also a basis for great love and excellence in relatedness.

Sports, games, and martial arts give us a highly ritualized way of engaging in competition and formalizing conflict. They structure relationships, and the play is supported by the precision of forms, strength of rules, and fair scorekeeping. This allows the players and spectators to participate in the thrill of rivalry without the destructive danger uncontained conflicts pose.

One of the most formidable fighters of all time, Muhammad Ali, was nominated for the Nobel Peace Prize. How can that be? The human spirit has great range. Like Ali, we can cultivate a deeply loving and peaceful heart and still step into the interpersonal ring with each other. But to do so requires clear intention. We need to consciously direct our communications and refine our skills so that fearlessness, flexibility, and play enter our relationships. Then we can elevate our game, so to speak.

In the realm of the awakened interpersonal, victory is not about dominating the other. Rather, it guides the transformation of opposing energies, our own as much as our opponent's. The intention to transcend opposition rather than prevail over the other makes all the difference. Energies with powerful destructive potential may be redirected to enliven us instead. Now that is a real victory. But it is not easy; we all must cultivate the skillful means to accomplish it.

It helps to keep sight of the fact that conflict is an expression of our profound and inextricable relatedness. We only conflict because we coexist. Buddhism holds that everything arises together in a mutually interdependent web of cause and effect. Conflict is one of the most direct ways to experience this profound mutuality, even though we rarely see it this way. Circumstances appear oppositional to us, dividing one from another. But conflict itself proves our ultimate inseparability.

Our recognition of this truth changes the way we respond to conflicts. We can no longer blame others or ourselves. We learn to engage our lovers, family, coworkers, neighbors, and, at the national and global level, even our political foes with a deep respect for the dimension in which we are the same. We really are defined by each other.

As we learn to bring greater wisdom and compassion to our conflicts, we naturally begin to choose the fights that really matter, while surrendering our petty, unnecessary, ego-driven conflicts more easily. This doesn't mean we won't have days of bad moods or reactivity, but the more we practice, the easier it becomes to find humor in our peevishness and to be more tolerant when others feel and act the same way.

Finally, all conflicts are a manifestation of the transience of all things. Martina and Chrissie's rivalry was, like all phenomena, impermanent. It is over and done, and it is now remembered not for who won or lost a particular title, but as a transcendent expression of the beauty of the game and the beauty of their uncommon friendship.

Recently I had a small blowup with one of my best friends. We yelled loud and long at each other about "insignificance and injustice" (whatever that meant), while my husband shouted platitudes from the safety of another room like "Girls, girls, calm down." I stomped out of the kitchen indignantly and thought for sure she had left. But when I strode back in a few minutes later, there she was, sitting in a chair like a composed Kanzeon Bodhisattva, reading a magazine. We looked at each other and chuckled. It's why we have been friends for more than thirty years. She demonstrated great fearlessness in engaging with me the way she did, and great faith in staying put. I demonstrated great skill in suggesting that we were both right. My husband, always a fair witness, showed the kind of fortitude that I admire in a man. After all, any man who remains calm when two women go at it is worth fighting for.

PRACTICE

Competition as Love

1. Who are the people in your life with whom you fight?
2. Who do you avoid fighting? Why?
3. Is there a worthy opponent in your life? Who do you trust to help you develop your skills?

22

Endless Practice

Satori is mistake after mistake.
IKKYU[1]

I HAVE MADE MANY MISTAKES in my life. Many. Lots of times I have earnestly attempted to communicate and only made matters worse. Sometimes I have offered what I thought was a helpful viewpoint and alienated a friend, colleague, or stranger. Once in a while, I have done my best to listen but have lost my temper instead. I don't find this conflict resolution business easy, except when I think about how other people could be doing it better than they are.

There are different ways to go about it. We can ignore the whole thing and withdraw from the challenge of relationships. Or, God forbid, we can imagine we are above it all, leaving just a faint scent of self-satisfaction wafting as we ascend to the realm of our superiority.

On the other hand, we can come out of the cave, down to the ground, or out from behind the wall of our cynicism and choose to participate in the dense, bruising activity of human interaction. We can see ourselves as part of an evolutionary process in which we, our practice, and our creative responses will continue to grow and evolve, freeing us at last from the unnecessary habits of quarrel or withdrawal.

Or perhaps we can do both. I wouldn't want to choose between the light in Ramana Maharshi's eyes or the depth in Abe Lincoln's face. For me, they are both expressions of divine truth. On an absolute level, Love is our natural state, requiring nothing from us at all except our recognition of it and a willingness to say, "All is well."

But from the relative or evolutionary point of view, we have work to do. It is imperative that we learn new skills, listen more deeply to different points of view, or learn to take a stand and speak with clarity of purpose when the issues of our day or the issues at home call us to do so. Our capacity for authenticity, genuine intimacy, and decent influence or effective social action are earned moment by moment through trial, error, commitment, and practice.

Learning communication, negotiation, and conflict skills takes time, patience, and effort. Practice requires a clear intention, lots of repetition, and a willingness to encounter the discomfort of the ego's resistance when its self-serving assumptions are challenged. Practice involves valuing others and their unique paths and perspectives, in spite of what we perceive as their limitations, errors, and obfuscations. Most important, we have to be willing to make our own dumb mistakes and, according to the old saw, "try, try again." Practice is, by its nature, endless, as all great Zen masters remind us: Our practice is our life.

Just Lose

When I was divorcing my first husband, I was mired in the distress of change. One night, overwhelmed by hurt, regret, anger, and uncertainty, I couldn't sleep. Then I heard a voice in my head say, "Just lose." The word *lose* had an immediate impact on me, far more than if I had heard the spiritual instruction to "surrender" or "let go."

I honestly didn't know I was engaged in a winning and losing proposition, but I saw that, in fact, I was. I was holding on with all my might—to my story, my injuries, and my preferences as to how our marriage, and now our divorce, should unfold. So I took that uncanny advice from nowhere, gave up my positions and cherished outcomes, and (at least momentarily) fell into my pillow and went to sleep.

I wanted my husband and me to stay on good terms, or as the folks in Hollywood say, "remain friends." But he wasn't cooperating. Being friends wasn't his thing. He was an artist with a demanding vision, intense discipline, and an imperative to work diligently on behalf of his vision. While he was socially skilled, he didn't care about that. As I said, not his thing. We were splitting up because it had become clear that we didn't share the same intention for our daily life. So why did I think we could find the harmony in divorce that we didn't find as a couple? I had to surrender my idea of how it should be between us.

Twenty years later, despite very few moments of personal exchange, we have raised our son with relative ease and mutual respect. We are not friends; his preference won out. But we are sound parents. It took getting divorced for me to let go of my ideas of how it should be between us. If I hadn't, I would resent him even today. "Just lose," I was told. "All right," I replied, often reluctantly, each time the resistance came up.

I have learned a lot from this practice of losing. Some conflicts, it seems, are not meant to be resolved, at least not in this lifetime. Some relationships will only be repaired in eternity, if then. It's mysterious how it all works, and nobody has the answer. The Dalai Lama has doubts about his response to the Chinese invasion of Tibet, sometimes wondering if they should have tried to put up a fight. Abraham Lincoln was assassinated in the very moment of victory over the bitter struggle against slavery. While the North won the war, preserving the Union, it was at such great cost that the battle still reverberates today. My Zen teacher, who was the closest person to me at one time in my life, is now the furthest away. How did that separation happen?

Why? Reasons abound but fail to explain. At least he and I each know the place beyond this coming and going.

How do we reconcile ourselves to that which doesn't resolve? We most often look at the world through a dualistic lens of winning or losing, coming or going, conflict or peace. That is the way we tell our stories. They have a beginning, a middle, and an end, and they revolve around conflicts. Conflicts create dramatic tension. The tension builds, complicates, and resolves. Finally, a gratifying denouement occurs. But that is art.

Our own lives don't conform to such a neat narrative structure. We can't get cooperation for the once-and-for-all happy ending; life itself continues to blend the happy and the sad, the up and the down, the victory and the loss, and finally comes to an end in what Leonard Cohen calls "our inevitable defeat."

How essential, then, to practice the surrendering now. This is how to understand the Buddha's words when he says, "Nothing whatsoever is to be clung to as I or mine. Whoever has realized this has realized all the teachings."

In this context of inevitable defeat and certain loss, there is great freedom. Through our surrender, compassion miraculously occurs; so does mercy, and so does tenderness. So we practice wholeheartedly, without fast and hard attachments to the outcomes. We soften our hearts, become a little more humble, keep extending ourselves to others, experience disappointment, and laugh over the absurdity of our efforts. All is well after all.

Willingness to Serve

With practice, we can develop our conflict skills. We learn to engage with awareness and compassion, and we are liberated from fixed outcomes. We discover fearlessness. Other people are not so intimidating anymore; difficult conversations are less threatening. We experience real success, and yes, it feels good.

Conflict confronts us with the need to change and to grow, and it provides the energetic boost to fuel that change. It catalyzes the expansion of our identity or demands that we change our life direction. We see that it is inherent to our creative process, and we are somehow grateful for it. And when there is no resolution, conflict becomes a doorway to acceptance of how things are and the humility of living in a universe as vast, mysterious, and unknowable as ours.

While we can develop an array of skills, each moment presents us with a choice: Am I going to listen now? Am I interested in seeing what they see, in feeling what they feel? Am I open to another perspective? Am I willing to let go of my attachment to how I think things should be? Or am I going to sidle back down the alley of myself and my opinions, to which I have grown so accustomed, and where I rule all alone?

Learning conflict skills will ask something of us. The more intimate we become with human suffering, the greater our compulsion to serve others. Just as the judge is inevitably paired with the criminal and the outcast, the doctor is joined with the sick and the dying, and the peacemaker is drawn to conflict. That is just the way it is. We don't have to heroically take the world upon our shoulders, but we might have to be willing to share our skills and understanding when the time comes. Service is the fulfillment of our practice; as the saying goes, it feels as natural as ripe fruit falling from a tree.

Self-Fulfilling Joy

I received another phone call from Willie recently. He seemed to be in a particularly buoyant mood, so I asked him, "What is it that is making you so happy this morning?" He replied, "It is my honor."

In his own unique way, he pointed out the happiness that is inherent in our being. It doesn't need to be earned, explained, or worked for. It is a joy that is always there, just below the surface, arising naturally when it is not obscured by our worries, our complaints, judgments, and struggles. Like bubbles rising to the surface of a champagne bottle, innate happiness simply needs to be uncorked and poured into a waiting glass. And like Willie, we are all privileged to do the pouring.

The practice of meditation will help us experience this fundamental well-being and joy. It teaches us to relax the grasping mind, to be present to how things are, and to see how everything is workable. Even in difficult circumstances or in times of challenge or conflict, we sense the underlying continuity of all of our experience, whether the mind labels it good or bad, right or wrong. We may even begin to see larger intelligence at work, or witness the goodness that pours out around all the pain and crisis in the world. We become accustomed to the tenderness of innate nature, and naturally appreciate our world, amidst all of life's inevitable ins and outs, ups and downs.

Examples of the innate goodness in our life are everywhere, available to see and appreciate. For me, I am reminded when I ask Willie how he is, and he looks up at me through smudgy glasses, making the A-OK sign with his pudgy fingers, and says, "I'm perfect." Or when I hear my father praising the potatoes he grew in his garden, as though the universe had given them to him personally to hand out. Or when my mother giggles when someone hands her a new baby to hold. It is really sweet. I appreciate it every workday morning, when my husband strides positively out the door, under the unruly weight of documents and legal briefs. "No reason to complain about being a lawyer," he says. "I am working at my desk, out of the rain and sitting down."

These things happen every day, all the time. Life is good, even when it is hard. So let's raise our glass like Hafiz suggests when he says,

Let's toast—
Every rung we've climbed on Evolution's ladder.
Whisper, "I love you, I love you!"
To the whole mad world.[2]

It is, after all, our honor.

Notes

CHAPTER 1: *Conflict Is Good News*

1. Hafiz, "Tired of Speaking Sweetly," *The Gift,* trans. Daniel Ladinsky (New York: Penguin, 1999), 187.

CHAPTER 2: *Inner Peace, Outer Peace*

1. Geshe Kelsang Gyatso, *Transform Your Life: A Blissful Journey* (Glen Spey, N.Y.: Tharpa Publications, 2007).

2. Eckhart Tolle, *The Power of Now: A Guide to Spiritual Enlightenment* (Vancouver, B.C.: Namaste Publishing, 1997), 12.

CHAPTER 3: *Intention: The True North*

1. Master Hsing Yun, *Describing the Indescribable*, trans. Tom Graham (Somerville, Mass.: Wisdom Publications, 2001).

2. Anousheh Ansari, "Interview with Anousheh Ansari," by Sara Goudarzi, *Space.com*, September 15, 2006, www.space .com/2889-interview-anousheh-ansari-female-space-tourist.html.

CHAPTER 4: *Attention and Awareness*

1. David Schiller, ed., *The Little Zen Companion* (New York: Workman Publishing Company, 1994), 17.

2. Zen Master Seung Sahn, *The Compass of Zen* (Boston: Shambhala Publications, 1997), 201.

3. Shunryu Suzuki, *Branching Streams Flow in the Darkness* (Berkeley, Calif.: University of California Press, 1999), 137.

CHAPTER 5: *Scary, yet Exciting*

1. From a calligraphy by Chögyam Trungpa, author's collection.

2. Chögyam Trungpa, *The Essential Chögyam Trungpa* (Boston: Shambhala Publications, 1999), 123.

CHAPTER 6: *Three Conflict Styles*

1. Mark Twain, ed. Charles Neider, *The Autobiography of Mark Twain* (New York: HarperPerennial, 2000), 155.

2. Thomas-Kilmann Conflict Mode Instrument, www.kilmann diagnostics.com.

CHAPTER 7: *The Marvel of Multiple Perspectives*

1. Carlos Castaneda, *A Separate Reality: Further Conversations with don Juan* (New York: Simon and Schuster, 1997), 154.

2. Ken Wilber, *A Theory of Everything* (Boston: Shambhala Publications, 2000), 71.

CHAPTER 9: *Speak for Yourself: The Importance of the First-Person Perspective*

1. Ken Wilber, *A Theory of Everything* (Boston: Shambhala Publications, 2000), 71.

2. Agnes de Mille, *The Life and Work of Martha Graham: A Biography* (New York: Random House, 1991), 264.

3. Marshall Rosenberg, *Nonviolent Communication: A Language of Life* (Encintas, Calif.: PuddleDancer Press, 2003).

CHAPTER 10: *Listening: The Art of Second Person*

1. Robert Fripp, *BrainyQuote.com*, www.brainyquote.com/quotes/quotes/r/robertfrip320731.html.

2. Ram Dass and Paul Gorman, *How Can I Help?* (New York: Knopf, 1985).

3. J. Krishnamurti, *The Collected Works of J. Krishnamurti: The Art of Listening* (Dubuque, IA: Kendall/Hunt Publishing, 1991).

CHAPTER 11: *Witnessing: Through the Lens of Third Person*

1. Lao Tzu, *Lao-tzu's Taoteching*, trans. Red Pine (Port Townsend, Wash., Copper Canyon Press, 2009), 32.

2. Bernie Glassman, *Infinite Circle* (Boston: Shambhala Publications, 2002), 140.

CHAPTER 12: *Everything and Nothing*

1. Ikkyu, *Wild Ways,* trans. John Stevens (Boston: Shambhala Publications, 1995), 51.

2. Chögyam Trungpa, *The Path Is the Goal* (Boston: Shambhala Publications, 1995), 107–8.

3. Rumi, "The Guest House," *The Essential Rumi,* trans. Coleman Barks (San Francisco: HarperOne, 2004), 109.

CHAPTER 13: *Negotiation*

1. Roger Fisher and William Ury, *Getting to Yes: Negotiating Agreement without Giving In* (Boston: Houghton Mifflin Harcourt, 1986), 23.

CHAPTER 14: *Conflict and Creativity*

1. Ken Wilber, from an unpublished transcript of a conversation on creativity with the author.

2. Ibid.

CHAPTER 15: *Reframing: The Power of Interpretation*

1. William James, from *The Principles of Psychology*, www.quotations page.com/quote/1971.html.

CHAPTER 16: *Giving and Receiving Feedback*

1. Chögyam Trungpa, *The Collected Works of Chögyam Trungpa*, vol. 8 (Boston: Shambhala Publications, 2004), 58.

2. Rumi, *The Essential Rumi,* trans. Coleman Barks (San Francisco: HarperOne, 2004).

3. David Schiller, ed., *The Little Zen Companion* (New York: Workman Publishing Company, 1994), 124.

CHAPTER 17: *The Shadow in Conflict*

1. C. G. Jung, "Good and Evil in Analytical Psychology," *The Journal of Analytical Psychology* 5, no. 2 (July 1960), 91–100.

2. Ibid.

3. Ken Wilber, *Integral Spirituality* (Boston: Integral Books, 2006).

CHAPTER 18: *Evolving Worldviews*

1. Ken Wilber, *Integral Spirituality* (Boston: Shambhala Publications, 2006), 6–7.

2. Rumi, "How Does God Keep from Fainting," *Love Poems from God: Twelve Sacred Voices from the East and West,* trans. Daniel Ladinsky (New York: Penguin, 2002), 77.

3. Saint Teresa of Avila, "When the Holy Thaws," *Love Poems from God: Twelve Sacred Voices from the East and West,* trans. Daniel Ladinsky (New York: Penguin, 2002), 290.

CHAPTER 19: *The Compassionate Heart*

1. Virginia Woolf, *Selected Works of Virginia Woolf* (London, U. K.: Wordsword Editions, 2007), 100.

2. Ibid.

3. Zen Master Dogen, *Shobogenzo: Zen Essays by Dogen,* trans. Thomas Cleary (Honolulu: University of Hawaii Press, 1986).

4. Hafiz, *The Gift,* trans. Daniel Ladinsky (New York: Penguin Books), 34.

CHAPTER 20: *Expanding the Heart*

1. Pema Chödrön, *Start Where You Are: A Guide to Compassionate Living* (Boston: Shambhala Publications, 1994), 38–43.

2. Ibid.

CHAPTER 21: *Great Rivalry, Great Intimacy*

1. Walt Disney, "Walt Disney Quotes," JustDisney.com, www.just
disney.com/walt_disney/quotes/quotes01.html.

CHAPTER 22: *Endless Practice*

1. Ikkyu, *Crow with No Mouth*, trans. Stephen Berg (Port Townsend,
Wash.: Copper Canyon Press, 1989), 31.
2. Hafiz, "If It Is Not Too Dark," *I Heard God Laughing: Poems of
Hope and Joy*, trans. Daniel Ladinsky (New York: Penguin Books,
2006), 27.

Bibliography

Chödrön, Pema. *Start Where You Are: A Guide to Compassionate Living.* Boston: Shambhala Publications, 1994.

Dass, Ram, and Paul Gorman. *How Can I Help?* New York: Knopf, 1985.

Dogen, Eihei. *Shobogenzo: Zen Essays by Dogen.* Translated by Thomas Cleary. Honolulu: University of Hawaii Press, 1986.

Fisher, Roger, and William Ury. *Getting to Yes: Negotiating Agreement without Giving In.* Boston: Houghton Mifflin Harcourt, 1986.

Glassman, Bernie. *Infinite Circle.* Boston: Shambhala Publications, 2002.

Gyatso, Geshe Kelsang. *Transform Your Life: A Blissful Journey.* Glen Spey, N.Y.: Tharpa Publications, 2007.

Hafiz. *The Gift.* Translated by Daniel Ladinsky. New York: Penguin, 1999.

Krishnamurti, J. *The Collected Works of J. Krishnamurti: The Art of Listening.* Dubuque, Iowa: Kendall/Hunt Publishing, 1991.

Mascetti, Manuela Dunn, ed. *The Little Book of Zen.* New York: Barnes and Noble, 2001.

Mindell, Arnold. *The Leader as Martial Artist: Techniques and Strategies for Revealing Conflict and Creating Community.* Zurich, Germany: Lao Tse Press, 2000.

Rosenberg, Marshall. *Nonviolent Communications: A Language of Life*. Encinitas, Calif.: Puddle Dancer Press, 2003.

Rumi. *The Essential Rumi*. Translated by Coleman Barks. San Francisco: HarperOne, 2004.

Saint Teresa of Avila. "When the Holy Thaws." In *Love Poems from God: Twelve Sacred Voices from the East and West*. Translated by David Ladinksy. New York: Penguin, 2002.

Thomas-Kilmann Conflict Mode Instrument. www.kilmanndiag nostics.com.

Tolle, Eckhart. *The Power of Now: A Guide to Spiritual Enlightenment*. Vancouver, B.C.: Namaste Publishing, 1997.

Trungpa, Chögyam. *Cutting Through Spiritual Materialism*. Boston: Shambhala Publications, 1973.

———. *The Essential Chögyam Trungpa*. Boston: Shambhala Publications, 1999.

———. *The Path Is the Goal: A Basic Handbook of Buddhist Meditation*. Boston: Shambhala Publications, 1996.

Wilber, Ken. *The Atman Project*. Boston: Shambhala, 1980.

———. *Integral Spirituality*. Boston: Integral Books, 2006.

———. *The Integral Vision: A Very Short Introduction to the Revolutionary Integral Approach to Life, God, the Universe, and Everything*, Boston: Shambhala Publications, 2007.

———. *Sex, Ecology, Spirituality: The Spirit of Evolution*. Boston: Shambhala, 2001.

———. *Spectrum of Consciousness*. Wheaton, Ill.: Quest Books, 1977.

———. *A Theory of Everything: An Integral Vision for Business, Science, and Spirituality*. Boston: Shambhala Publications, 2001.

———. *Up from Eden*. Wheaton, Ill.: Quest Books, 1981.

Index

About the Author

DIANE MUSHO HAMILTON is a gifted mediator, facilitator, and spiritual teacher. She has an uncommon ability to address the challenges of our modern experience within the context of timeless wisdom. With extraordinary warmth, depth, and insight, Diane encourages us to consciously evolve beyond limited ideas of who we are so that we may manifest our unique expression of insight and compassion.

Diane is well known as an innovator in facilitating group dialogues, especially conversations about culture, religion, race, and gender. She was the first director of the Office of Alternative Dispute Resolution for the Utah judiciary, where she established mediation programs throughout the court system. She is the recipient of several prestigious awards for her work in this area, including the Peter W. Billings Award and the Utah Council on Conflict Resolution's Peacekeeper Award.

She has studied and practiced Buddhadharma for almost thirty years, beginning at Naropa Institute in 1984 with the teachings of Chögyam Trungpa Rinpoche. She was ordained as a Zen priest in 2003 and received dharma transmission from Genpo Merzel Roshi in 2006. She is a facilitator of Big Mind Big Heart, a process developed by Roshi to bring the insights of Zen to Western audiences. She has collaborated with the Integral Institute and Ken Wilber since 2004, developing the Integral Life Practice seminars and the Integral Spiritual Experience, and teaching to Integral audiences throughout the world.

With her husband, Zen teacher and lawyer Michael Mugaku Zimmerman, she established the Two Arrows Zen, a center for the study and practice of Zen meditation in Utah. They maintain two centers: one in downtown Salt Lake City and another in the red rock country of southern Utah, where meditation is complemented by nature practices and wilderness exploration.